BIBLICAL CHRISTMAS PLAYS AND MUSICALS

Plays, Musicals, Songs, Skits and Tableaux

Compiled by Rebecca Daniel

Illustrated by Corbin Hillam

Cover by Janet Skiles

Shining Star Publications, Copyright © 1989

A Division of Good Apple, Inc.

ISBN No. 0-86653-513-6

Standard Subject Code TA ac

Printing No. 98765432

Shining Star Publications
A Division of Good Apple, Inc.
Box 299
Carthage, IL 62321-0299

TO THE TEACHER/PARENT

Biblical Christmas Plays and Musicals is a book that allows students the rare opportunity to become part of the greatest story ever told—the birth of our Lord, Jesus Christ. Customs, culture, and everyday feelings that the people in that period of history experienced can be shared by each and every student.

Have you been searching for a unique way to present the Christmas story to your class? Consider a play or musical! Creative drama is the perfect way to involve your students and show them a realistic portrayal of Bible times. Each of the eight plays, seven musicals, seventeen original Christmas songs, skits, and tableaux, set in Biblical times, has been written especially for young performers. The joyous, singable songs can be incorporated into the plays to extend them into musicals or can be used alone as musical presentations. Any way you choose to mix and match the numerous plays, musicals and songs, you are sure to receive a standing ovation when you present the original and unique Bible-based dramas included herein!

Reproducible playscripts and musical scores, a special costuming unit, tips for directing and production, and mask and scenery patterns, all are guaranteed to make your Christmas performance hassel free. This Christmas give each of your Bible students the best Christmas gift of all, the joy of knowing (experiencing) the true meaning of Christmas!

TABLE OF CONTENTS

DEDICATION

When the heavenly choir of angels sang
There was a catastrophe,
For a new little angel had joined the group
And he always sang off key.
So the choir of angels talked it out
And decided that if it must be,
They would love and include the small cherubim
Even though he sang off key.
On Christmas Eve when the choir rejoiced
And sang their songs of glee,
The small chirpy angel perched on the Star
And happily sang off key.

by Dorothy Edgerly Zimmerman

CHRISTMAS PLAYS

TIPS FOR PLAY DIRECTORS

When presenting your play(s), the following instructions may be helpful:

1. Begin by reading many plays to the children to find out which one they enjoy the most. Let the youngsters help decide which play they will perform.

2. Once you have selected the play you will be performing, the scriptural account of the drama should be studied by all prospective cast members and after casting, before rehearsals begin.

3. Reread the play with the children, making sure they understand the meaning of all words and have some idea of the background of the characters.

4. Selecting the cast can be done by rereading the play as various children read or repeat lines. Listen for their interpretation of certain characters before selecting the cast. Even those players portraying stars, animals, etc., can develop their characters into ones that have distinct personalities. Encourage creativity whenever and wherever possible.

5. When parts have been selected, make sure the young people emphasize how each participant in the story felt about what was happening. This will help them develop a particular mood and feeling in their presentation.

6. Children must memorize before rehearsal. Practice the speaking parts in small groups offstage several times before actually going to the stage to practice.

7. Do not tire the children with long rehearsal periods. Shorter rehearsals over a longer period of time aid in producing better results. We want dramatization to be a joy, not a task.

8. A dress rehearsal the day before the final performance will help insure a smooth presentation.

Shining Star Publications, Copyright © 1989, A division of Good Apple, Inc. SS1871

A CHERISHED HOPE COMES TRUE

by Lucille B. Golphenee

Cast of characters:

Mary, Joseph, Baby Jesus, Three shepherds, Angels

(A few sheep may be cut from poster paper or cardboard. See patterns on pages 93-96 or children may be dressed as lambs.)

Narrator:　Reads Luke 2:1-8.

Scene I

(Three shepherds are out watching their sheep—Amos, his father and Marcus. Lights dim.)

Amos:　Well, Father, how are you feeling tonight?

Father:　Not too good, son. Not too good. My bones are growing old and weak. If only I could live to see the Messiah, I could die in peace.

Marcus:　Do you think that time is drawing near?

Father:　Yes. The prophets long ago foretold His coming. I think it should be very soon now.

Amos:　You just take it easy, Father, and rest. Marcus and I will tend to the sheep. Isn't that right, Marcus?

Marcus:　Yes, that is right. We will see to everything.

Father:　Thank you both. I will lie down right here, on my blanket, where I will be handy if needed.

Curtain.

Narrator:　Reads Luke 2:9.

Scene II

(Angel appears. Bright light goes on angel. Shepherds shrink back in fear.)

Angel:　Fear not, for behold I bring you good tidings of great joy, which shall be to all people. For unto you is born this day in the city of David a Saviour, which is Christ the Lord. And this shall be a sign unto you; Ye shall find the babe wrapped in swaddling clothes, lying in a manger.

(More angels appear.)

Angels:　Glory to God in the highest, and on earth peace, good will toward men.

(Angels all disappear. Men are silent for a moment.)

Father:　Blessed be the Lord God of Hosts. The wonderful event has happened. The Messiah has come.

Marcus:　Wasn't that a strange and great happening? I was much afraid at first.

Amos:　Yes, it was marvelous. I, too, was frightened until the angel spoke. Then my fear left me.

Father:　We must make haste and go see this Saviour who has been born.

Amos:　But, Father, do you think you can make the trip? It will be very tiring for you.

Father:　Yes, I must go. This is what I've been living for all these years. It is the thing I must do before I die. God will help me.

Amos:　We will help you along also, Father, and you can rest when you grow weary.

Marcus:　Yes, we will assist you all we can.

Father:　You are both a great comfort. Come, let us go at once.

(Amos and Marcus each take one of Father's arms, and they start out.)

Curtain.

Narrator:　Reads Luke 2:15-16.

SS1871

Scene III

(Mary and Joseph are in the stable. Baby Jesus lies in manger.)

Joseph: How are you feeling now, Mary?

Mary: I am fine, Joseph, but very weary.

Joseph: It has been a hard trip on you, and you must rest all you can for our return journey.

(Suddenly a knock comes at the door.)

Joseph: I wonder who that could be? *(Goes to door and opens it. The shepherds stand just outside.)*

Joseph: Ho, strangers! Who are you, and what do you seek?

Marcus: We are but humble shepherds, sire, and we would see the newborn Saviour.

Amos: Angels came with a great light, and told us the glad tidings.

Father: Yes, we would see Him. He is the Messiah, foretold by prophets of old. He is the Saviour of the world.

Joseph: Do come in. You are welcome.

(Shepherds enter the stable.)

Joseph: This is my wife, Mary. We have come from afar, and she is quite weary.

Mary: *(Smiles.)* The baby lies yonder in the manger.

Father: God be with you, kind lady.

(Shepherds go to manger and look down at baby.)

Father: I would be greatly honored if I may take Him in my arms for one moment.

Mary: Yes, you may. He is a very good baby.

(Father picks up baby and looks down at it lovingly, then bows head and prays.)

Father: I thank You, Heavenly Father, for allowing me to see your Salvation before I die.

Curtain.

Narrator: Reads Luke 2:17-20.

Scene IV

(Shepherds step outside and prepare to leave and go back to their sheep.)

Marcus: Such wonderful happenings! I can scarce take it all in!

Amos: He looked so peaceful,—and somehow glorious.

Father: He is the great King and Redeemer of the world. We must tell all our friends of His wonderful birth.

Amos: Would you like to rest for a while before we return to the sheep, Father? You must be very weary.

Father: Son, I feel better than I have in years. Just seeing the Christ Child has renewed my strength. I thought I would be ready to die after seeing the Messiah, but now I feel I could live forever.

Amos: That is wonderful news, Father. Shall we take your arm?

Father: I thank you, but I am quite able to walk alone now. Glory be to the God of our Fathers.

Amos and
Marcus: Amen and amen.

Curtain.

RICHES AND RIDDLES

by Virginia L. Kroll

Cast of characters:
Sami, the prince   Susannah
Shepherd   Mary
Asher   King
Ben   Children

Playing Time: 10 minutes

Setting: A stable (Scene I) and the outdoors (Scene II)

Costumes: (Scene I) Sami and King wear lavish, colorful robes and crowns adorned with jewels. Shepherd wears a long brown robe belted at waist. Mary wears a loose blouse, shawl, veil, and long skirt in white and blue combinations. (Scene II) Sami and the children wear simple (for example, burlap) sacks.

Properties: A manger for the stable, a doll, a stick, a lamb, a beanbag, wood or cardboard doors for stalls, a backdrop to represent the outdoors, and several cutout rocks and bushes.

Lighting: No special effects.

Sound: No special effects.

Scene I

Time: Daytime, shortly after the first Christmas.

Setting: The stable

(At Rise: Sami sits at center stage, drawing on the floor with a stick. Shepherd enters, carrying a lamb. He kneels before Sami.)

Shepherd: Oh, holy prince, I worship you most humbly. I have brought you a newborn lamb, the prize of my flock.

Sami: (Standing up.) Stop, sir! You make me quite uncomfortable. I am not the prince you seek.

Shepherd: (Surprised.) Not the prince? (Gets up slowly.)

Sami: No. That is, I am a prince, but I am just an ordinary prince. (Points to manger.) There is the Prince whom you came to worship.

Shepherd: (Puts hand to forehead in a searching gesture and looks around stable in all directions.) Where? I see no prince but you.

Sami: There, in the manger.

Shepherd: (Walks over and looks into manger.) Why, that is no prince. That is a common babe without even a proper bed. He is beginning just like any ordinary man.

Sami: That is why He will be the greatest prince of all.

Shepherd:	You are baffling me with your puzzles. How can I believe such things?
Sami:	Faith will make you know. His light shines for miles around and draws visitors here.
Shepherd:	The light! That is what compelled me here. Then it is His light? (*Points to manger.*)
Sami:	His very own. (*Shepherd places lamb in front of manger, kneels with head bowed, and exits. Ben, Asher, and Susannah enter. They bow in front of Sami.*)
Susannah:	Oh, sweet prince, we have come to pay you homage.
Sami:	(*Putting his hands to his head and shaking it with annoyance.*) This happens over and over. Please do not embarrass me so. I am not the prince you seek.
Asher:	We followed a light. It led us here. We heard there was a boy prince. We must be mistaken.
Sami:	You are not mistaken.
Asher:	You talk in riddles. First you say we are mistaken, then you say we are not.
Sami:	Your Savior the Prince is indeed here. (*Children look all around.*)
Ben:	Where? I see no other prince.
Sami:	There, in the manger.
All Children:	(*Shocked.*) The manger? (*They walk over and look into crib.*)
Ben:	This baby is the prince?
Sami:	Yes. His mother is at the market, and her husband is in the pasture. I am tending Him while they are gone.
Susannah:	Well, what about you? If you are not a prince, why do you look like one?
Sami:	Actually, I am a prince. I am just not *the* prince.
Ben:	(*Throwing both hands up.*) I'll never understand this!
Asher:	Where is your kingdom?
Sami:	Far, far to the East. I, too, saw the star and followed it. I traveled with my father and two other kings.
Susannah:	(*With awe.*) Then you *are* a real prince. We beg your pardon, for we should not be in your royal presence. (*To Ben and Asher.*) Brothers, come.
Sami:	Oh, please, don't go.
Asher:	We must. It isn't proper. We are sorry to have disturbed you, your highness. (*Children turn to leave.*)
Sami:	(*Sharply.*) Stay! (*Children jump and turn back.*)
Asher:	(*Looking around furtively.*) Well, just for a moment, as long as no one catches us.
Ben:	Can I touch your crown?
Susannah:	(*Reprimandingly.*) Ben!
Sami:	(*Laughs.*) Of course, here, you may wear it. (*He takes the crown off and hands it to Ben.*)
Ben:	(*Turning crown over with awe.*) I've always wanted to wear a crown. Sometimes I pretend that I'm a prince.
Sami:	Put it on then; now is your chance. (*Ben puts on the crown and stands up very straight.*)
Ben:	How do I look?
Susannah:	You look like Ben with a crown on. Now quickly, take it off before someone sees.
Sami:	Why? It is no crime to try on a crown.
Susannah:	It just isn't proper, that's all.
Ben:	(*With disappointment.*) Oh, it's all right. (*He removes the crown.*) Wearing a crown doesn't make me a prince anyway.
Sami:	And taking it off doesn't make me *not* a prince. We are what we are on the outside, but we may be something altogether different on the inside.

Asher:	You are telling us another riddle.
Sami:	(*Laughs.*) It is easier to understand than it sounds.
Ben:	(*Throwing both hands up.*) I'll never understand!
Sami:	Look at the child yonder. (*Indicates manager.*) He wears no crown, yet He is the highest prince of all.
Asher:	Still, your expensive jewels and fine clothing make us feel uncomfortable.
Sami:	As your bowing makes me.
Asher:	But you are royalty, and we are common folk.
Sami:	Do you deny that I am a boy like you?
Asher:	(*Hesitating.*) Well . . . no.
Sami:	And must boys bow to one another?
Ben:	(*Throwing up both hands.*) I'll never, ever understand this!
Susannah:	(*Cupping her ear in a listening gesture.*) Shhh. I hear footsteps approaching. We must go. (*She takes one brother by each arm and the children exit together.*)
Sami:	(*Taking a few steps after them.*) Do come back. Please! (*Goes and stands over manger.*) Oh holy Prince, I wish You were a little older so that You could help me explain. Why can't people accept the fact that underneath all my furs and jewels and silk, I am just a normal boy? They are so blinded by the glitter that they do not see what is beyond it. What good is owning jewels if one does not have friends? What good is wealth that isn't shared? (*Walks a few steps with head down, then turns slowly.*) But of course! (*Looks into manger.*) I will become like You. I will remove the blinding glitter and let my goodness shine through on its own to lighten and warm the hearts of those I meet. (*Mary enters.*)
Mary:	We are back. Joseph is unhitching the mules. Were there any visitors?
Sami:	Yes, four. A shepherd and three children.
Mary:	(*Picks baby out of manger and cuddles him.*) Did the child give you any trouble?
Sami:	Trouble? Oh no! He gave me ideas.
Mary:	(*Laughs.*) Ideas?
Sami:	Yes, the best ideas I've ever had. Now I must go and put them into practice. (*Sami exits. Quick curtain.*)

Scene II

Several hours later outdoors. Sami is standing off to one side. The children are tossing a beanbag back and forth to one another. It drops near Ben. As he picks it up, he notices Sami and pauses a moment.

Ben:	(*To Susannah and Asher.*) Look, there's a boy over there. (*To Sami.*) Hey, come play with us. (*To Susannah and Asher.*) If we have another player, we can have teams. (*Sami joins the group.*) You can be my partner. (*They separate into two teams. Ben throws beanbag to Asher. Asher throws it to Sami. Sami throws it to Susannah. She is standing with her hands at her sides, staring at Sami, so the beanbag falls in front of her. Ben and Asher look in confusion at each other and at her and shrug.*)
Asher:	What is it, Susannah?
Susannah:	It is the prince.
Ben:	At first I thought so too, but he wears no crown, no jewels. He cannot possibly be the prince, but a mere look-alike.

Asher:	(*Staring at Sami.*) But he is, in fact, the prince.
Sami:	And so I am.
Ben:	We asked you to play because we thought you were an ordinary boy.
Sami:	And so I am.
Susannah:	(*Smilingly conceding.*) And so you are.
Sami:	Now, will you be my friends?
Asher:	If you will be ours.
Sami:	I shall! I shall! (*They resume the beanbag toss.*)
King:	(*Offstage.*) Sami . . . Sami . . . Where are you? (*Enters.*) Oh, here you are. (*The children huddle together.*)
Sami:	You know me, Father?
King:	Of course I know you.
Sami:	But how do you recognize me?
King:	(*Laughs.*) Recognize you? I would know you anywhere! You are my son.
Sami:	(*To children.*) You see? Even without my jewels and my silk and my furs, I am still who I am.
King:	But who are these common children?
Sami:	They are my friends.
King:	Friends? Indeed! Do they understand that you are a prince? Do you understand that they are not royalty?
Sami:	We understand what is important, Father.
King:	Where did you get such strange ideas?
Sami:	From the Babe, whose light brought us here.
King:	The Babe? Son, you talk in circles. You make me quite dizzy. Get your coat and come to the tent. It is time to dine.
Sami:	Father, I have no coat.
King:	You have several of fine furs.
Sami:	I gave them to the street dwellers who shiver through the night.
King:	And your jewels? Where are your precious emeralds? Your sapphires? The pearls?
Sami:	I have given them to the widows and orphans whose stomachs ache from hunger.
King:	And your crown? Where is your regal crown?
Sami:	A prince owns it now.
King:	Your tricky tongue is causing my mind to spin again. Explain yourself.
Sami:	I have given it to the newborn prince.
King:	But we already bestowed upon Him spices and perfumes.
Sami:	Those were your gifts, Father. The crown is mine. If anyone deserves to wear it, it is a prince.
King:	You are a prince.
Sami:	I never said I was not a prince.
King:	But how unlike a prince you act! You have nothing now. You have given it all away. You are poor.
Sami:	Not at all, Father. Before, I merely owned things like jewels and furs and money. Now, I am rich.
King:	My son, you put me to the test. And your riddles are quite beyond me. But since they are a part of you, I have no choice but to accept them.
Sami:	And what of my friends? They are part of me, too.
King:	(*Rubbing his chin thoughtfully.*) My son, you are wealthy in wit. You have tricked your poor father into seeing the truth. Come, we will discuss all this at the table as we dine, (*King opens his arms*) along with your worthy friends. (*Children and Sami go to King, two on each side. King puts his arms around their shoulders. All exit together.*)

 SS1871

RUTH WAS THERE

by Lucille B. Golphenee

Cast of characters: Ruth and Miriam

Scene: The two girls are sitting in the living room, talking.

Ruth: I am so glad you have come to stay with us a few days, cousin Miriam. It has been such a long time since we have seen each other, and I have so much to tell you.

Miriam: Nothing exciting ever happens in my life. It is different for you and your folks here at the inn. You meet all kinds of people. It must be very interesting.

Ruth: That is true, but this is something very special that has happened.

Miriam: Go ahead and tell me quickly. I am very anxious to hear your story.

Ruth: Well, it was some time ago, really, but it seems like it was just yesterday. It was when everyone had to come and pay their taxes. There were so many people here for lodging, that we were crowded full to the brim.

Miriam: Yes, I remember. Father and Mother had to pay taxes too, but go on.

Ruth: A young couple, named Joseph and Mary came to the inn. Mary was about to have a baby. We had no room for them in the inn, so Father let them take shelter in our stable.

Miriam: It surely is too bad your inn was too full to take them in.

Ruth: Yes, it was. I felt very sorry for Mary. She looked so worn out and half sick. After they were settled, Mother let me take them some food and fresh water. They were famished, and so thankful for the refreshments.

Miriam: That was very nice of you and your Mother.

Ruth: I was worried about them and went back that evening to see if I could do anything to make them more comfortable. This is the really exciting part. (*She pauses.*) Mary had already had her baby.

Miriam: She had! So soon?

Ruth: Yes, He was wrapped in swaddling clothes and lying in the manger asleep. Even the cattle and sheep were quiet. It was as if they didn't want to awaken the little one. It was so peaceful, the place seemed somehow, well, holy.

Miriam: How very strange!

Ruth: Then suddenly someone knocked at the door. Joseph went to answer it, and there were three men standing there. He asked who they were and what they wanted. They said they were humble shepherds come to see the newborn Saviour of the world.

Miriam: Saviour of the world!

Ruth: Yes. And they said a bright and shining angel came and told them about it. They said they were very frightened.

Miriam: My, my, I should think so!

Ruth: But the angel said not to be afraid, and said he brought them good news of the Saviour of the world being born that day in the City of David, and they should find Him wrapped in swaddling clothes and lying in a manger.

SS1871

Miriam:	It was Him alright then, wasn't it?
Ruth:	Yes, it was. Then more angels came and said, "Glory to God in the highest, and on earth peace, good will toward men.
Miriam:	My! I have never heard of such a thing before!
Ruth:	It never had happened before. When the angels left, the shepherds came and found the place as the angel had said.
Miriam:	Then what happened?
Ruth:	Joseph let the shepherds in, and they came up to where the Baby lay, and kneeled down and worshipped Him.
Miriam:	They worshipped Him?
Ruth:	Yes, and when they left, they said they were going to tell all their friends of the wonderful Baby. And I guess they did, because a lot of people heard and wondered at it.
Miriam:	How exciting! I wish I could have been there.
Ruth:	After the shepherds had left, I asked Mary if I might hold the Baby. She smiled and said I could, and Joseph laid Him in my arms, and the Baby smiled.
Miriam:	He did?
Ruth:	Yes, and I can't tell you what a wonderful feeling it gave me to hold Him in my arms. I asked Mary what His name was, and she said an angel had come and told her she was to have the Baby, and to call Him Jesus.
Miriam:	An angel! Imagine that!
Ruth:	I wished they could stay forever, but of course they couldn't. But there is still more.
Miriam:	Have you seen them since then?
Ruth:	No, but I heard some time after they had left, that wise men from the East came to see Him. They said He was to be King of the Jews, and they said they had seen His star in the east, and it had gone before, and led them to the place where Jesus lived.
Miriam:	How did they know it was His star?
Ruth:	I think they had studied the stars, and God probably told them, too. They knelt before Him and worshipped Him. Also, they brought expensive gifts— gold, frankincense, and myrrh for the newborn King.
Miriam:	(*Sighs deeply.*) Is there any more to tell?
Ruth:	No, but I'm sure there will be if He is to be a king, and Saviour of the world.
Miriam:	If you hear any more of Him, be sure and let me know.
Ruth:	I will, but you will probably hear too, as I'm sure He is going to be very well-known. Now I think Mother is calling me to help her with the guests. (*Arises.*)
Miriam:	I will go along and see if there may be something I can do.
Ruth:	Thank you. I'm sure there will be.
Miriam:	(*Following Ruth from room, murmurs wonderingly.*) His name is Jesus, King of the Jews—Saviour of the world.

Curtain.

THE LAST NAME
by Marilyn Senterfitt

Cast of characters:

Joseph	Anna
Roman Officer	Mark
Adam	Ruth

Costumes: Long robes, headcoverings, sandals

Props: table, chair, scrolls, quill or pointed stick, small clay container

Setting the scene: Place table and chair stage center. On table, set one scroll unrolled, the quill and clay container. Other scrolls may lay on floor or be put in a basket by the table.

(*Play begins with Roman Officer seated at table. Adam and Anna stand before him. Mark and Ruth stand stage right. Joseph enters stage left and stands behind Adam and Anna.*)

SS1871

Roman Officer: What is your name?

Adam: I am Adam. I own several profitable vineyards.

(*Roman Officer "writes" on the scroll as information is given. Occasionally dips quill in container.*)

Roman Officer: What tribe?

Adam: The tribe of Reuben.

Roman Officer: Your wife's name?

Adam: She is Anna.

Roman Officer: Any children?

Anna: Four. They are called Joshua, Samuel, Joel and Sarah.

Roman Officer: All right. Now just move on.

(*Joseph moves forward and Adam and Anna join Mark and Ruth. They pretend to carry on a conversation.*)

Roman Officer: Will this census never end? Next!

Joseph: I was not able to come earlier. The child was born last night.

Roman Officer: Are you staying at one of the inns?

Joseph: No, we arrived too late. The innkeeper gave us a place in the stable. That is where the babe was born.

(*The men and women begin to listen to Joseph and the Roman Officer.*)

Roman Officer: Your name?

Joseph: I am Joseph, a carpenter from Nazareth.

Roman Officer: What tribe?

Joseph: The tribe of Benjamin and David. We are descendants of kings.

Roman Officer: All you Jews think you are kings. There is only one king and he is Caesar. Because of him I sit here writing useless information on a scroll. Your wife's name?

Joseph: Mary.

Roman Officer: And the child?

Joseph: He is called Jesus. It means the Saviour of the people.

Roman Officer: So you say. (*Reads aloud as he writes.*) Jesus, son of Joseph, of the tribe of Benjamin. Now move on. Perhaps I'll yet get a hot meal this day.

(*Joseph moves to leave. The men and women walk toward him. Mark takes hold of Joseph's arm.*)

Mark: Did you say the child will be Saviour of the people?

Adam: He didn't say that. He only said that was what the child's name means.

Joseph: But it has been foretold that this child is the Messiah.

14

SS1871

Ruth: Last night I was drawing water from the well and several shepherds came up to me. They were excited and talking about angels and seeing the Messiah in a manger. Was this your child?

Joseph: Yes, those shepherds did come to the stable and they worshipped the Babe.

Adam: Wait! You expect us to believe that the long-promised Messiah was born in a stable in this wretched town?

Joseph: Yes, it is true.

(*Adam and Anna laugh out loud.*)

Anna: God would not choose such a dismal place for His Son to come to this earth. He would be born to a queen in a palace.

Mark: I, too, heard the shepherds when they spoke to my wife. They believed they had seen the Messiah.

Adam: What do shepherds know? Angels speaking to shepherds . . . this is all make-believe!

Joseph: You may see the child if you wish. I know Mary will not mind.

(*Adam takes Anna's arm.*)

Adam: My wife and I have better ways to spend our time.

(*They exit stage right.*)

Mark: Ruth and I would be honored to visit the child.

Ruth: I would first like to stop at our house. We would want to take a gift to the child.

Joseph: That isn't necessary.

Mark: Oh, but we want to!

Joseph: You are very kind. We will go to your house and then we shall go to the stable together.

(*Joseph, Mark and Ruth exit stage left.*)

Roman Officer: I believe I have finally completed this census. What was that last name? (*Reads from scroll.*) Jesus, son of Joseph, of the tribe of Benjamin. (*Laughs aloud.*) It is a dream to think a babe born in Bethlehem could become King of the Jews. Just a wild dream.

(*Roman Officer rolls up scroll. Picks up quill, clay container and the other scrolls. He exits stage right.*)

SS1871

THE WISE MEN'S CAMELS

by Marilyn Senterfitt

Cast of characters: Three camels—Ali, Ben and Baba

Costumes: On three 11″× 14″ pieces of white poster board draw the faces of camels. Cut out circles for child to see through. On back, attach two loops made of poster board strips to either side of cutout. Children will hold the loops as they "look out" the circle and speak their lines.

Ben: I don't know about you two, but my footpads are weary.

Ali: Mine also. This has been a very long journey.

Baba: I wonder where we are.

Ali: I heard my master call the place Bethlehem.

Ben: It certainly isn't much of a town.

Baba: But this is where the star led us. See how it shines right over the town.

(*All three look up at the sky.*)

Ali: We have followed that star for many months.

Ben: At least we travelled by the cool of the night.

Baba: Do you really think the king our masters seek will be in this lowly place?

Ben: I thought surely our journey was over when we came to Herod's palace. Wasn't the hay delicious in that stable?

Ali: Oh, yes, it was, but I think my master did not have a good feeling about that King Herod.

Baba: Did you see all the gold my master brought for the newborn king?

Ali: Yes, but it hardly compares to the bottle of precious myrrh my master will give to him.

Ben: My master's gift of frankincense is most certainly worthy of a king.

Baba: I still find it hard to believe a king has been born here.

Ben: This must be the place. Our masters are far too wise to make such a mistake as that.

Baba: You are right! This must be our destination and the end of our long journey.

Ali: Our masters will have much to tell when we return home.

Ben: So will we!

SS1871

THE SHEPHERD'S LITTLE BOY

by Katherine D.M. Marko

Cast of characters:

Father
Mother
Grandmother
Little boy, Isaac, about six years old

Mary
Joseph
Narrator

(*Soft music of "Silent Night" is heard.*)

Narrator: (*At the side of the stage.*) On the night of Jesus' birth, shepherds were watching their flocks as usual on the hills outside Bethlehem. Suddenly a bright light shone above them and angels appeared.

Scene I

(*A room in a shepherd's house, with a window on one side. Through the window a light is shining. Beneath the window there is a narrow bed on which the boy, Isaac, is lying. There also is a crib in the corner, and a table and two chairs in the middle of the room. Door is opposite window. Drapes hang across the back as divider between two rooms.*)

Isaac: (*Standing on his bed, he looks out the window.*) Oh, it is like daytime outside. (*A loud knock on the door is heard. Isaac lies down quickly and pulls the covers over his head.*)

Mother: (*In nightdress and robe, she hurries into the room through the drape divider and lights a lamp. Another knock is heard. She goes to the door.*) Who is it?

Father: (*Calling from outside.*) Open the door, Sarah. It is I, Caleb.

(*Isaac sits up in bed and listens silently.*)

Mother: (*Opening the door.*) Caleb! Is something wrong? Why have you left the sheep?

Father: (*Coming in.*) Nothing is wrong, but something wonderful has happened.

Mother: At this time of night?

Father: Yes, angels appeared in the sky and sang to us.

Mother: Angels? (*Drawing back, she puts up her hands.*)

Father: Don't be afraid. They told us not to fear.

Mother: But why did they come?

Father: To tell us that a new king had been born who is the Saviour of the world. He must be the Messiah.

   SS1871

Mother:	A king? But where?
Father:	In Bethlehem in a stable. They said the child would be lying in a manger.
Mother:	Oh, my goodness, a stable. How strange that the Messiah would be born in a stable.
Father:	The town is crowded. The inn would have no room.
Mother:	Well, a stable is shelter at least, but which one?
Father:	The one behind the inn would be the most likely one. The other shepherds and I are going there now. Eben's son is watching the flocks until we return.
Mother:	(*Going to the table.*) Would you like something to eat before you go?
Father:	No, the others are waiting for me on the road. (*He turns to the door.*)
Mother:	Well, be careful. It is cold tonight. (*She closes the door behind him.*)
Isaac:	Mother, can we go to see the baby King?
Mother:	(*Pulling her robe tightly around her.*) We'll see in the morning. Now go back to sleep. We mustn't wake little Simon. (*Isaac lies down and Mother tucks him in and blows out the lamp.*)

(*Light shows through the window.*)

Isaac:	It's like daytime outside.
Mother:	Yes, there is a huge star in the sky. Now go to sleep. (*She exits through drape divider.*)

Curtain.

Narrator:	(*At side of the stage.*) This story is like many Christmas legends which can't be proven true or untrue. But since the shepherds were the first ones to hear about Jesus' birth, something like this could have happend.

Scene II

(*Same setting as Scene I. It is the next morning. Little Isaac is still sleeping. There is a pitcher, a cup and a plate on the table; also a large tray filled with loaves of bread. Mother, standing at the table, slices a loaf. She places the slices on top of other loaves and covers all with a towel.*)

Mother:	(*She checks the baby in the crib, then goes to Isaac and touches his shoulder.*) It is time to get up, Isaac. But be quiet. Little Simon is still sleeping.
Isaac:	(*He sits up in bed and looks at the window.*) Is it morning?

Mother:	Yes, it is morning.
Isaac:	Where did the light from last night go?
Mother:	I told you it was a star. You can't see stars in daytime.
Isaac:	(*He gets up and pulls on a shirt.*) Now can we go to see the baby King?
Mother:	(*Smiling.*) I see you remember. Yes, we may go to see Him.
Isaac:	(*He goes to the wall peg and reaches for his cloak.*) When?
Mother:	(*Putting up her hand.*) Not yet. You must eat first and then we have to wait for Grandmother to come and stay with little Simon.
Isaac:	All right. I'll eat fast.
Mother:	No, you must not get sick. (*She gives him a slice of bread on the plate and pours some milk into the cup.*) The bread is still warm from the oven.
Isaac:	(*Sitting down.*) Could we take some bread to the baby King?
Mother:	Yes, I intend to. (*She wraps two loaves in a towel.*)
Grandmother:	(*Just entering the door.*) My, my, we're up early. (*She pats Isaac's head.*)
Isaac:	Mother, now can we go?
Grandmother:	Go where? (*She hangs up her shawl.*)
Mother:	Caleb came in last night with exciting news. Angels appeared to the shepherds and told them a king had been born in Bethlehem. (*She smiles.*) We are going to see Him.
Grandmother:	Angels? Why should angels announce the birth of a child?
Mother:	The child must be the Messiah. And the great star we saw must be a sign.
Grandmother:	I'm sure it was. (*She clasps her hands together.*) A sign that He has come at last. How wonderful!
Isaac:	(*He rises from the table and pulls on his cloak.*) Hurry, Mother.
Mother:	Patience, son. (*She puts on her cloak and takes up the wrapped loaves. Then she leans over the crib, kisses the baby and turns to Grandmother.*) We won't be long. Come, Isaac. (*They leave.*)

Curtain.

| Narrator: | (*At side of the stage.*) The stable where the animals of the innkeeper were kept was bare of human necessities, but it was shelter from the cold winter weather of Judea. |

Scene III

(*Mary and Joseph stand at either side of the manger, smiling and patting the child lying on the hay in it. Large poster board cutouts of an ox and a sheep are placed at the side of the stage opposite the door. (See patterns on page 93.) Mother and Isaac poke their heads in through the doorway.*)

Mother:	May we come in?
Joseph:	Please do.
Isaac:	It's nice and warm in here.
Mother:	Yes, it is good.
Isaac:	(*Looking at Mary and Joseph.*) May we see the baby King?
Mary:	(*Smiling, she nods to Isaac.*) Yes, you may.
Mother:	(*She goes to Mary and hands her the bread.*) A little gift.
Mary:	Thank you.
Mother:	(*Kneeling at the manger, she leans forward to see the baby.*) How beautiful. (*She gently pulls Isaac down beside her.*)
Isaac:	(*He stretches his neck, then tugs at Mother's cloak.*) I can't see Him.
Mother:	(*She helps him to his feet.*) Can you see Him now?
Isaac:	(*Excitedly.*) Yes, I can see Him, I can see Him.
Mother:	Shhh.

(*Mary picks up the baby, kisses Him and holds Him up in plain view.*)

Isaac:	What is His name?
Mary:	He is called Jesus.
Isaac:	(*He stares for a long moment, looks towards the door, back to the child, then away and back again.*) He is different.
Mother:	Yes, now shhh. (*She bows her head. Isaac looks at the child, then away and back again. Mother rises.*) We must go now.

(*Mother bows to Mary and Joseph and takes Isaac's hand. They back away toward the door, then turn and exit.*)

Scene IV

(Same setting as Scenes I and II. Mother and Isaac enter. Grandmother stands near the baby's crib. Mother takes off her cloak and helps Isaac out of his. After hanging them on the wall peg, she rubs her hands together to warm them.)

Mother:	It is good to come in where it is warm.
Isaac:	It sure is cold out there.
Grandmother:	*(Clasping her hands.)* Did you see Him?
Mother:	Oh, yes, He is beautiful.
Grandmother:	How wonderful.
Isaac:	The baby's name is Jesus.
Grandmother:	*(Patting Isaac's head.)* Oh, so you found out His name?
Isaac:	Yes, but He was just a baby. He didn't have a fancy chair like a king. He didn't even have a bed.
Mother:	No, He's not like other kings.
Grandmother:	He is a heavenly king.

(Isaac goes to little Simon in the crib, and looks down at him. He looks away, then back and away again.)

Mother:	Isaac, what are you doing?
Isaac:	I'm looking at Simon.
Mother:	But why are you turning your head like that? You did the same thing at the stable.
Isaac:	Mother, did you think the baby in the stable looked different?
Mother:	Yes, of course.
Isaac:	But why?
Mother:	*(Smiling.)* He is God.
Isaac:	*(He looks down at little Simon again. Then he claps his hands and bounces up and down.)* Now I know. Now I know.
Mother:	Shhh, not so loud. What do you know?
Isaac:	I know what's different.
Mother:	About the baby Jesus?
Isaac:	Yes, Simon is just an ordinary baby, but the baby King has a light around His head.
Mother:	That is a halo. *(She hugs Isaac.)*

(Little Simon cries. Grandmother picks him up and hums to him. Soft music of "Silent Night" or "Jesus Is Sleeping," page 82, is heard.)

Curtain.

Narrator:	*(Stepping in front of curtain.)* May the joy that came to little Isaac come to all of you this Christmas Day.

Shining Star Publications, Copyright © 1989, A division of Good Apple, Inc. SS1871

JEHU'S CHAIN

by Lucille B. Golphenee

Cast of characters:
Mary
Joseph
Baby Jesus
Jehu

Yusuf
Yusuf's mother
Three shepherds

Scene I

Narrator: A young boy, Jehu, is seen lying on the ground, with only a thin blanket over him. He is shivering with cold, and trying to go to sleep. His mother and father are both dead, and he is forced to beg for a living. Let us listen in as he talks to himself and prays.

Jehu: (*Turning restlessly.*) Oh, how I wish Mother had not died. I get so lonely I can hardly stand it. (*Clasps his hands and bows his head as he prays.*) Dear God, I know I am just a little beggar boy, but I need help. Please help me find Mother's sister that she has told me so much about. I have tried so hard, but I am about to give up. Thank you, God. Amen.

(*Closes his eyes for a minute, then opens them again.*)

Jehu: Hark! I hear voices. (*Raises up on one elbow to listen. Three shepherds enter scene.*)

First Shepherd: I can hardly wait to see the newborn Saviour.

Second Shepherd: Wasn't it just wonderful when the angels appeared and told us of His birth?

Third Shepherd: The angel said we would find Him wrapped in swaddling clothes and lying in a manger. How strange for the Saviour of the world.

First Shepherd: The ways of God are wonderful and beyond our understanding.

Jehu: (*Rising up.*) A Saviour is born! I must go and see Him too. (*Walks toward shepherds.*) Please, kind sirs, may I go along with you? I too, would see this newborn Saviour.

Second Shepherd: Yes, do come along, lad. We will enjoy your company.

Jehu: (*He is silent for a minute, then talks to himself.*) But I should have a gift for the wonderful Saviour. I have nothing but these rags I am wearing, and my old torn blanket. (*Pauses and puts his hand to his head.*) I know! I forgot this gold chain I wear around my neck, that Mother gave me just before she died. (*Pulls it out from where he has it hidden beneath his robe.*) This will make a fine gift for the wonderful child.

Curtain.

Scene II

(*Mary and Joseph are standing in the stable, looking down at baby Jesus, while the three shepherds kneel before Him. Animals may be cut from poster board or cardboard. See patterns on page 93. Jehu is standing just outside the stable. Another boy appears.*)

Yusuf: (*Sees Jehu standing hesitantly.*) Ho! Who are you and why are you here? I am Yusuf, the innkeeper's son.

SS1871

Jehu:	My name is Jehu, and I have come to see the newborn Savior.
Yusuf:	Savior! I do not know anything about a Savior. There is a couple here with a newborn baby. I am here to see if they need anything. They have come from afar, and must be hungry.
Jehu:	I was lying on the ground, trying to sleep, when three shepherds came along and said they were going to see the newborn Savior that the angels told them about. I was set on seeing Him myself, so I came with them. They are in there now. They said He is to be the Savior of the world.
Yusuf:	That is very strange and wonderful news.
Jehu:	I have nothing to give Him but this gold chain that my mother gave me before she died. She said I should try to find her sister, and she would surely know who I was by the chain, as she had given it to her just before she was married. (*Takes the chain from around his neck and shows it to Yusuf.*)
Yusuf:	That is beautiful! May I show it to my Mother? She loves jewelry. I promise to bring it back soon.
Jehu:	(*Hands Yusuf the chain.*) Yes, I trust you. You may take it. I will wait here for you.

Curtain.

Scene III

(*Yusuf is in the inn, talking to his mother.*)

Yusuf:	(*Holding out the gold chain.*) Look Mother! Isn't this a lovely chain?

(*Mother looks, then examines it. She puts her hand to her head, and the other hand over her heart.*)

Mother:	Yusuf, please bring me a drink of water. I feel faint.
Yusuf:	Mother! What's wrong? (*He hurries to bring water. She takes two or three swallows. Takes the cup and leads her to a chair.*)
Mother:	That chain! (*She gasps, looking at it lying in her hand.*) I'd know it anywhere. It has a heart pendant inscribed, "With all my love." I gave it to my long lost sister just before she married. Wherever did you get it?
Yusuf:	A boy out by the stable had it. He said his mother gave it to him just before she died.
Mother:	Oh no! My poor dear sister. Please bring the lad in, Yusuf.

(*Yusuf leaves room and comes back with Jehu. Jehu stares at Yusuf's mother, then rubs his eyes, and looks again.*)

Yusuf:	What is it, Jehu? What's wrong?
Jehu:	I, I thought for a minute my mother had come back. They look just alike.
Mother:	Come lad, what is your name, and where are you from?
Jehu:	I am Jehu, and I have walked far to get to the place of my mother's birth to look for her sister she talked so much about.
Mother:	(*Leaning forward eagerly.*) And what was your mother's name, lad?
Jehu:	Her name was Leota, ma'am.
Mother:	(*Wiping her eyes.*) Now I know of a surety that she was my sister. It breaks my heart to know I have lost her for good, after all these years. But why did we not ever hear from her?

Shining Star Publications, Copyright © 1989, A division of Good Apple, Inc. SS1871

Jehu:	My father was a drinker, and we were very poor. She was too ashamed to let you know. He died in an accident, and after that, Mother was sick for some time, and finally died, too.
Mother:	(*Puts her hands over her eyes to hide her tears.*) Oh, how awful! My poor darling sister. But you are her son. I am glad that you finally found us. You must live here with us, and you will be another son to us.
Yusuf:	And you will be my brother. Isn't that great? I have always wanted a brother. (*He puts his hand on Jehu's shoulder and Jehu wipes his eyes.*)
Jehu:	It is almost too wonderful to be true. God has answered my prayers. Now I must go see the newborn Saviour, and give Him my gold chain.
Mother:	Saviour, did you say? We did not know who He was, or we would have let them have our bed. But are you going to give Him your precious chain?
Jehu:	Yes, it is all I have, and the man said He is to be the Saviour of the world.
Mother:	That is great news indeed. I must look into this more closely.
Yusuf:	I will go with you, Jehu.
Mother:	You must take them something to eat and drink. (*Hands Jehu the chain.*) Wait up. (*Goes into other room and brings food on a tray.*) Here, give them this little lunch and fresh water. They must be famished after their long journey.

Curtain.

Scene IV

(*The shepherds have gone, and Mary and Joseph are seated beside baby Jesus. Jehu and Yusuf enter.*)

Yusuf:	See, I have brought you food and drink. Eat, and be strong again for your journey home.
Mary:	Thank you kindly, lad, and God bless you and yours. We are quite famished.
Jehu:	May we see the wonderful baby?
Mary:	Surely. He is lying there in the manger. (*Both boys go and look.*)
Yusuf:	He looks so peaceful. I'm sure He will be a great man.
Jehu:	(*Holds out chain to Mary.*) Here is a gift for the baby. It is all I have to give. Mother gave it to me just before she died.
Mary:	That is very kind of you, but you must not give away your precious chain, lad. (*Looks at his shabby clothes.*) You could sell it and buy new garments for yourself.
Jehu:	(*Shakes head vehemently.*) Oh no! I would never sell it, but I want to give my best to your wonderful son. What is His name?
Mary:	The baby's name is Jesus. When He gets old enough, I will tell Him about the lad who loved Him so much, he gave Him all he had.
Yusuf:	Jehu is going to live with us from now on, and be my brother. He really is my cousin who just found us.
Mary:	That is wonderful. The Lord bless you both.
Jehu:	Now I must thank God for answering my prayers. (*They all bow their heads.*) Thank you, God, from the bottom of my heart for hearing me, and helping me, and letting me see the wonderful Saviour of the world. Thank you again. Amen.

(*Hidden choir begins to sing softly, "O Little Town of Bethlehem" or "The Angels Sang," see page 77.*)

Curtain.

THAT NIGHT
by Marilyn Senterfitt

Cast of characters: Joel and his father, Aaron

Costumes: Both wear long, loose-fitting robes with headcoverings. Aaron carries a crook or wooden stick. To distinguish his age, Aaron may have a beard. They both wear sandals.

Setting the scene: At stage center lay down a large green cloth. Construct a pile of rocks with wire mesh or chairs. Cover with a brown cloth. Potted trees and shrubs may be added for color. Place stuffed lambs or cutouts (*see patterns on page 93*) around the rocks.

(*Aaron enters stage left walking with his crook. Joel follows close behind. Aaron sits down at base of rocks and Joel sits nearby.*)

Aaron: I'm beginning to feel the cold more than when I was young. (*Motions as if trying to get warm.*) Are you enjoying your first night as a shepherd, son?

Joel: Yes, Father! I have waited a long time for this day.

SS1871

Aaron:	I told you you could join me in tending the flock as soon as you had your twelfth birthday .
Joel:	Would you tell me again about that night?
Aaron:	(*Smiling.*) You never tire of hearing it and I never tire of telling it.
Joel:	It is so exciting! Is this close to where it happened?
Aaron:	This is the very spot!
Joel:	(*Awed.*) Oh! The angels spoke to you here?
Aaron:	Yes, on a night just like this, thirty years ago. I was but a boy of fourteen and I remember every detail of that night.
Joel:	Tell it again, Father!
Aaron:	Your grandfather, seven other men and I had just settled the sheep for the night. There was not a whisper of wind and the sky was full of stars. We had all noticed one especially bright star, but shepherds have little interest in such things.
Joel:	I know about that star!
Aaron:	Yes, now we all know it led those kings to Bethlehem, but that night it was just another bright star in the nighttime sky.

*(*Aaron could sing solo: "O Lovely Star," see page 84.*)

Joel:	Who saw the angel first?
Aaron:	Actually, I did. I was standing my watch while the others slept, which is what you will be doing shortly, Joel. Anyway, I realized that something strange was happening. The whole area was becoming brighter and brighter. The shadows around the hills were disappearing. Then I saw it.
Joel:	The angel!
Aaron:	Yes, I cried out and the others jumped to their feet ready to battle an intruder. Then they also saw the angel. We were very afraid.
Joel:	Were you truly afraid, Father?
Aaron:	Yes, I was! We fell to the ground and thought we were surely going to die. Then the angel spoke.
Joel:	I know the words. "Fear not: for, behold, I bring you good tidings of great joy, which shall be to all people. For unto you is born this day in the city of David a Saviour, which is Christ the Lord. And this shall be a sign unto you; Ye shall find the babe wrapped in swaddling clothes, lying in a manger."

*(*Joel could sing solo: "Message to the Shepherds," see page 79.*)

Aaron:	Yes, exactly. We could not believe our ears and then the light grew even brighter as the other angels appeared.
Joel:	And they sang!
Aaron:	A chorus of angels singing to lowly shepherds. Their voices echoed among these hills. "Glory to God in the highest, and on earth peace, good will toward men."

*(*Aaron could sing solo: "Glory, Glory," see page 67.*)

Joel:	Oh, I wish I had been there!
Aaron:	Then they were suddenly all gone. The only sound was the call of a lamb for his mother. Your grandfather was the first to speak. He said we should go down to Bethlehem and see this Babe.
Joel:	I would have run all the way!
Aaron:	(*Smiling.*) We wanted to, but first we had to put the sheep in that old shelter over there. (*Points stage left.*) Then we did hurry down to Bethlehem.
Joel:	Bethlehem was crowded because of . . . What was it called, Father?
Aaron:	The census. Yes, it was quiet when we arrived. Most people were asleep in their beds. The streets and courtyards were lined with the donkeys and horses of the travelers. That bright star cast a strange light on the city.
Joel:	How did you know where to begin looking for the Babe?
Aaron:	Your grandfather thought we should try the inn that was built near the birthplace of King David. An old woman was standing by the entrance to the courtyard and Grandfather asked her if a Baby had been born in the inn.

*(*Aaron could sing solo: "What Can It Be?" see page 68.*)

Joel:	And she said yes, we could find him in the stable.
Aaron:	Right. We entered the stable and there was a man and woman and the Babe wrapped in soft white cloths lying in a hay-filled manger.
Joel:	Just as the angel had said! What did the Baby look like?
Aaron:	I have always found it hard to put into words. He was beautiful but in a wondrous way. We all fell to our knees and worshipped Him. I shall never forget it. We didn't stay long and soon returned to the flock, but on the way we told everyone who would listen about what we had seen and heard that night.

*(*Aaron could sing solo: "Who Is This Baby?" see page 69.*)

Joel:	Father, what do you think has become of the Baby?
Aaron:	He is a grown man now and I feel in the depths of my soul that we will soon be hearing from Him.
Joel:	I hope I get to see Him! Do you think I will even know Him?
Aaron:	Yes, Son, I believe you will not have a doubt if you get to meet the Saviour. Now it is time for you to stand your watch. Here, take my crook. (*Hands it to Joel.*) Will you be afraid alone on watch?
Joel:	Oh no, Father. I will be remembering that night long ago and those thoughts will keep me strong.

(*Joel exits stage left. Aaron looks up to the sky.*)

Aaron:	O, Lord, wherever your Son is this night, watch over Him and give Him strength. My prayers go with Him always.

(*Aaron stretches out on the ground and goes to sleep.*)

*(*Aaron could sing solo: "The Angels Sang," see page 77.*)

*See special notes on turning this play into an operetta.

DAVID TOUCHED THE SAVIOUR

by Lucille B. Golphenee

Cast of characters:

Mary	His father, John
Joseph	Peter
Baby Jesus	Laban
Angels	Sheep may be cut from poster board or cardboard
Young David	

Scene I

(*Shepherds are out with their sheep.*)

Father: David! Oh David! Come here at once!

David: (*Appears on the scene. Hangs head in shame.*) Yes, Father.

Father: I saw you this time. How often must I tell you that sheep are not built to be ridden like donkeys? You will hurt their backs.

David: But Father, it is so much fun.

Father: For you perhaps, but not for the sheep. Now let's have no more of it.

David: All right. (*Walks away and disappears.*)

Father: If only we could have some peace and quiet around here. Don't know what I am going to do with that boy. I don't like to punish him all the time. Talking seems to do no good.

Peter: Yes, it is a problem alright.

Laban: It is not good for the sheep to be disturbed so much.

Narrator: Time passes, and the shepherds settle down to watching the sheep.

Father: I wonder where David disappeared to. I haven't seen him around for some time.

Peter: He left right after you lectured him.

Laban: (*Points.*) I saw him head out that way.

Father: Probably sulking from my talking to him as I did. Think I'd better go looking for him. There may be wild animals around.

Peter: I will help you search.

Laban: I had better stay with the sheep, in case he comes back.

(*Father and Peter leave.*)

Narrator: Time passes again as the two men search for the boy. Finally they reappear.

Father: Has he not shown up yet?

Laban: No, there has been no sign of him.

Peter: We looked everywhere we could think of, without any results.

Father: (*Wiping his brow worriedly.*) I fear for the lad's life.

(*Suddenly David appears on the scene.*)

David: Hello, Father.

Father: Hello yourself! Where have you been all this time? Peter and I searched and searched for you. We were worried sick.

David: Oh, I just went down to the valley and did a little exploring.

Father: You did, eh? Well, next time you go exploring, ask permission first, and tell us where you are going.

David: (*Hangs head.*) I'm sorry, Father. (*Walks away and disappears.*)

Father: Boys! I declare, I don't know which way to turn.

Narrator: There is quiet for a while as the shepherds watch their sheep. Suddenly one of the sheep not seen on the stage gives out a loud "Baa."

Father: Now what's up? It's that David again! (*He calls.*) David!

David: (*Appears on the scene.*) Yes, Father.

Father: What have you been up to now, boy?

Shining Star Publications, Copyright © 1989, A division of Good Apple, Inc. SS1871

David:	Aw! I just pulled old Blackie's tail a little to see what he would do.
Father:	I am disappointed in you, David. A good shepherd does not hurt his sheep. We named you after the David in the Bible, hoping you would be a good shepherd like him. He loved his sheep and cared for them tenderly. Now go and try to be the kind of boy God wants you to be.
David:	I'll try, Father. (*Turns away slowly.*)

(*Turn lights down as night and darkness comes on. An angel appears on the scene, with a bright light shining on him. David runs and hides behind a bush, large rock or any large object. The men also throw up their hands in fright.*)

Angel:	Fear not: for, behold, I bring you good tidings of great joy, which shall be to all people. For unto you is born this day in the city of David a Saviour, which is Christ the Lord. And this shall be a sign unto you; Ye shall find the babe wrapped in swaddling clothes, lying in a manger.

(*More angels appear.*)

Angels:	Glory to God in the Highest, and on earth, peace, good will toward men. (*Angels could sing, "Message to the Shepherds," page 79.*)

(*Angels disappear. David peeks around the bush, then comes up to his father.*)

David:	Father, what does this all mean? I was so afraid I nearly died.
Father:	We, too, were frightened, lad. But this is great news. The Saviour of the world is born. The Messiah, foretold by prophets long ago.
Peter:	We must go and see this great king that has come to pass.
David:	May I go too, Father? I want to see this wonderful newborn baby. Please, may I, Father?
Father:	(*Strokes his beard thoughtfully.*) Yes, you may come along, son, if you will behave.
David:	Oh, I will, Father! I will!
Father:	No more pranks then?
David:	No more pranks. I promise.
Father:	Then let us go at once. (*They all start out walking.*)

Curtain.

Scene II

(*Mary, Joseph and baby Jesus are in stable, with Mary sitting down, and Joseph standing. Baby Jesus lying in manger.*)

Mary:	Is the Baby asleep, Joseph?
Joseph:	I can't tell. He is lying quietly with His eyes closed.
Mary:	He is such a precious Child. He hardly ever cries.
Joseph:	That is a great comfort after all you've been through.
Mary:	Yes, and I am very thankful to God for it.

(*Mary could sing, "Jesus Is Sleeping," page 82.*)

(*There is a knock at the door. Joseph goes to open it, but calls out first.*)

Joseph:	Ho, strangers! Who is there, and what do you want?

(*The shepherds are standing outside the door.*)

Father:	We are shepherds from the nearby countryside.
Laban:	We have come to see the newborn Saviour of the world.
Peter:	An angel came and told us about Him. He said we would find Him wrapped in swaddling clothes, and lying in a manger. This must be the place.

Joseph:	(*Opens the door.*) Yes, it is. Come on in. (*Sees David.*) You too, young man. What is your name?
David:	My name is David, sir.
Joseph:	That is a good name. I hope you will always live worthy of it.
David:	I'll try, sir.

(*The shepherds advance, and Mary starts to stand up.*)

Father:	Keep your seat, lady. We have just come to see your wonderful Baby. You must be very tired after your long journey.
Mary:	(*Sits down again.*) Yes, thank you kindly. I truly am quite weary. The Baby Jesus lies over yonder in the manger.

(*The shepherds go to the manger and kneel down in front of the baby. David crowds behind and tries to look over their shoulders.*)

David:	I want to see the Baby too, Father.
Father:	Yes, son. (*The shepherds step back and David goes up to the manger and looks down at the baby. He reaches over and touches baby Jesus, wonderingly.*) Your Son is a wonderful boy. I'm sure He will do great things when He grows up.
Peter:	Yes, thank you for granting us the privilege of seeing Him.
Laban:	He is a very special baby.

(*The three shepherds start to leave.*)

Father:	Come, David. We must go now.

(*David is still standing looking down at baby Jesus. He turns slowly, and goes to his father, as if in a trance, still looking back. They all go out the door.*)

Curtain.

Scene III

(*Shepherds are standing outside the door of stable.*)

Father:	I thank God for letting us see the Messiah.
Peter:	This has been the most wonderful night of my life.
Laban:	I will never forget it as long as I live. We must tell all our friends.
Father:	Well, David, you are very quiet. What do you think of the Christ Child, son?
David:	I touched Him, Father! I touched Him! I touched the Saviour of the world! He opened His eyes and looked at me.
Father:	Why, David, you are very serious.
David:	It was as if He said, "Go and be a good boy, David. Grow up to be a kind shepherd." And I'm going to, Father! I'm going to be like the Bible David, and do what God wants me to do.
Father:	That is wonderful news, son, and it makes my heart truly glad. No one who touches the Saviour of the world will ever be the same again. Now let us go back to our sheep.

Curtain.

(*Hidden choir sings "Silent Night," or any of the Christmas songs found on pages 66-71 or pages 74-84.*)

SKITS AND TABLEAUX

Skits and tableaux (a tableau is a depiction of a scene, usually presented on a stage by silent and motionless costumed participants) lend themselves much better to small numbers of people where groups are limited. The three selections that follow can be done with as few as two or as many as eight people. Here are several tips to make your performance inspirational:

1. Keep in mind that many speaking parts may be combined or divided to accommodate smaller or larger numbers of players than the cast of characters calls for.

2. Encourage young people performing the skits or tableaux to be as creative as possible. Encourage them not to be limited by the stage directions written into the scripts themselves. Have them suggest to whoever is directing the action what sort of movements and facial expressions feel most comfortable for them. Encourage creativity whenever and wherever possible.

FORETOLD

A Series of Christmas Tableaux
by Edith E. Cutting

Stage directions: The stage is divided so that one tableau can be prepared behind a curtain while the other is being presented. The scenes are as bare as possible so that all attention is focused on the characters and on the Biblical readings. All characters are silent. The only sounds are from the Narrator at one side in front of the stage and from the choir at the opposite side. The choir sings one verse of each indicated hymn after the Narrator reads. Although the King James Version of the Bible is best known, the New International Version may be easier for a student to read.

Narrator (*Before Scene I.*): At Christmastime we celebrate the birth of Jesus. The coming of Christ, the Messiah who would save the world, had long been foretold, though people had different ideas of what He would be like. What a joy it is that the advent of the "anointed one," as He was also called, was the birth of a baby, a very special Baby!

SS1871

Scene I

(*A young woman holding a baby or doll to represent the Baby.*)

Narrator: Hundreds of years before Jesus was born, Isaiah prophesied: Isaiah 7:14. Also he said: Isaiah 9:2,6.

Choir: "O Come, O Come, Emmanuel" or "I Am Bethlehem!" see page 66.

Scene II

(*As many children as possible crowded onto the stage, dressed in various costumes with make-up or masks to represent different races and ages.*)

Narrator: Listen now to the promise from Isaiah that the coming of the Messiah should be for all people. Isaiah 49:1, 6.

Choir: "We've a Story to Tell to the Nations."

Scene III

(*A big old tree stump made from brown wrapping paper or papier-mache with one evergreen branch rising from its side.*)

Narrator: Isaiah also foretold that the Messiah, the Christ, would come from the family of David, the youngest son of Jesse, and would bring a new and better world into being. Hear his announcement: Isaiah 11:1-6 and 9:7.

Choir: "Hail to the Lord's Annointed" or "The Angel's Greeting," see page 76.

Scene IV

(*Zacharias in long dark robe, with angel in white robe before him.*)

Narrator: Now we come to the New Testament, and the foretellings to special people. First was foretold the birth of John the Baptist, who was to come before Jesus and help prepare the way for Him. Zacharias, a priest in the Temple in Jerusalem, was promised that he and his wife, Elisabeth, even though they were old, would still have a son. Luke tells us the story. Luke 1:11-14, 18-21, 57, 67-68, 76.

Choir: "Master, Speak! Thy Servant Heareth"

Scene V

(*Mary kneeling before Angel Gabriel in white robe.*)

Narrator: Before the child John was yet born, the angel came also to the young Mary of Nazareth, telling her that she would bear a special child. Hear the story as Luke tells this part of it. Luke 1:26-35, 38.

Choir: "Angels We Have Heard on High" or "The Angel's Greeting," see page 76.

Scene VI

(*Older woman, Elisabeth, kneeling before Mary who is standing.*)

Narrator: Then Mary went to visit her cousin Elisabeth, who was to be the mother of John. When Elisabeth greeted her, Mary told her of the power of God. Luke tells us of her awe and wonder. Luke 1:46-55.

Choir: "Come, Thou Long-Expected Jesus" or "Mary Praises the Lord," see page 75.

Scene VII

(*Joseph asleep on pad on floor with angel in white standing near.*)

Narrator: Now Joseph, the man Mary was to be married to, became concerned about her, for he did not know what God had planned. He did not know whether he should marry her or not, but an angel of the Lord appeared to him in a dream and reassured him. Hear how Matthew tells the story: Matthew 1:18-25.

Choir: "Holy Spirit, Truth Divine" or "Joseph's Song," see page 70.

Scene VIII

(*Shepherds sitting together as spotlight shines down on them.*)

Narrator: At last came the time so long foretold, when this special Child was born. The first people to whom the birth was announced were the shepherds in the field near Bethlehem. Luke tells the story: Luke 2:8-14.

Choir: "While Shepherds Watched Their Flocks" or "Message to the Shepherds," see page 79.

Scene IX

(*Wise men kneeling before Mary and Baby.*)

Narrator: The Magi, or wise men, had studied the heavens and seen a beautiful, unknown star. Following that star, they finally arrived in Bethlehem to see the Baby who was born to be a King. Matthew tells their story. Matthew 2:1-12.

Choir: "We Three Kings" or "The Wise Men," see page 81.

Scene X

(*John in coarse short robe, facing several men in better robes.*)

Narrator: Jesus grew to manhood, as did his cousin John, the child born to Zacharias and Elisabeth. Now John, referring to the prophecy in Isaiah, again foretold Jesus' mission. Hear how Matthew tells what happened. Matthew 3:1-2, 5-6, 11.

Choir: "There's a Voice in the Wilderness Crying."

Scene XI

(*John and Jesus standing together, as if talking.*)

Narrator: And now we come to the moment when Jesus was specifically acknowledged, the time when all that had been foretold was verified. Here is Matthew's report. Matthew 3:13-17.

Choir: "Strong Son of God, Immortal Love."

Scene XII

(*Same as Scene I, Mary and Baby.*)

Narrator: So we celebrate the wonderful birth of Jesus, the Christ, the Messiah, the Son of God, whose coming was foretold hundreds of years before it happened and has been retold by the faithful ever since. Let us rejoice and do as Mary did, for Luke says, Luke 2:19.

Choir: "Hark! the Herald Angels Sing" or "Mary's Lullaby," see page 71.

Narrator leads audience to join in second and third verses.

ALPHA-BIBLICAL CHRISTMAS

by Dee Leone

This short skit for young children can be presented by itself or incorporated into a longer Christmas program. Each child can be assigned a separate letter of the alphabet. (Note—You can assign more than one letter to some of the children if desired.) Costumes and props for each letter can range from the very simple to the more elaborate. In the simplest form, each child can hold a poster with the letter of the alphabet and a corresponding picture. An option is to use a stick mask or a prop which goes with each child's line. (For example, a stick mask of an angel's head or an angel ornament can be used by the child assigned the letter "A.") If desired, children may dress in the full costume of the character or object mentioned after each part.

Setting—In the simplest versions of the play, children can stand in alphabetical order with their posters, stick masks, or props. They can step forward or take center stage when it is time to deliver their lines. If children are dressed in full costume, they can be positioned to depict a Nativity scene. They can remain in their places to deliver their lines. A manger with hay can be at center stage.

All:	(*Sing the following to the tune of "The Alphabet Song."*)
	Long ago on Christmas Day,
	In a stable full of hay,
	Baby Jesus laid His head.
	A lowly manger was His bed.
	Now we'll tell you of the birth
	Of Christ who came to save the earth.
A:	*A* is for the angels singing on high.
	Their songs of praise filled the sky. (Angel.)
B:	*B* is for Baby Jesus asleep upon the hay.
	He was born on Christmas Day. (*Mary pointing to Baby*.)
C:	*C* is for the camel, that brown, friendly beast
	Who brought the wise men from the East. (*Camel*.)
D:	*D* is for the donkey, who, uphill and down,
	Carried Mary to Bethlehem town. (*Donkey*.)
E:	*E* is for the eastern star
	Which led the wise men from afar. (*Star*.)
F:	*F* is for the frankincense one king did bring.
	He laid it before the newborn king. (*King bearing frankincense*.)
G:	*G* is for the gift of gold,
	Bright and shiny to behold. (*King bearing gold*.)
H:	*H* is for the hay in the manger bed.
	It made a soft place for Jesus to lay His head. (*Shepherd or cow with hay*.)

   SS1871

I: *I* is for the innkeeper who turned Mary and Joseph away.
All the rooms were full that day. (*Innkeeper standing off to one side.*)

J: *J* is for Joseph who went up from Galilee.
He traveled to Bethlehem because of Caesar's decree. (*Joseph.*)

K: *K* is for the kings who came from afar.
They found the Baby Jesus by following a star. (*All three kings.*)

L: *L* is for the light of Christ divine.
Let it shine. Let it shine. (*Angel holding a flashlight "candle."*)

M: *M* is for Mary, mother of the Child
Lying in the manger so tender and so mild. (*Mary.*)

N: *N* is for the Nativity scene which recreates the birth
Of the Saviour Jesus, born to save the earth. (*Angel, sheep or shepherd.*)

O: *O* is for the Orient from whence the wise men came.
Melchior, Gaspar, and Balthasar some say were their names. (*Camel.*)

P: *P* is for "Peace on Earth."
The angels said this at Christ's birth. (*Angel.*)

Q: *Q* is for the quiet night
When shepherds wondered at the sight. (*Shepherd.*)

R: *R* is for the Redeemer born to save us all,
Baby Jesus sweet and small. (*Shepherd pointing to baby.*)

S: *S* is for the stable animals who
Were witness to the miracle, too. (*Cow, sheep, or any stable animal.*)

T: *T* is for the treasures brought by the kings.
A gift of myrrh was among those things. (*King with myrrh.*)

U: *U* —Unto you is born this day
A Saviour you'll find in a manger full of hay. (*Angel.*)

V: *V* is for the virgin chosen as the one
To give birth to God's own son.
(*The same Mary or one kneeling off to the side with an angel standing near.*)

W: *W* is for the "watch by night"
Which shepherds were keeping when they took fright. (*Shepherd.*)

X: *X* is for Christmas with the word Christ left out.
Those who call it this are missing what Christmas is about. (*Angel.*)

Y: *Y* is for the yuletide cheer
Spread at Christmastime each year. (*Angel.*)

Z: *Z* is for Zacharias whose son, John, was born in ancient days.
John went before the Lord to help prepare His way. (*Shepherd.*)

All: (*Sing the following to the tune of "The Alphabet Song."*)
Long ago on Christmas Day,
In a stable full of hay,
Baby Jesus laid His head.
A lowly manger was His bed.
Now we've told you of His birth.
Spread the news throughout the earth.

Shining Star Publications, Copyright © 1989, A division of Good Apple, Inc. SS1871

THE CHRISTMAS STORY
by P.M. Keith

"The Christmas Story" can be presented in numerous ways:

1. Group may be divided into Choir 1 and Choir 2, each speaking certain assigned parts, then the entire group speaking on certain lines or parts.

2. Stanza-a-child is more difficult, as the timing must be perfect from one person to the next.

3. Part-speaking is used when different groups take parts of the selection.

4. Solo and chorus uses various members of the group speaking certain lines and then they join together to speak in unison.

5. Unison speaking is the most difficult way of presenting this poem. The entire group speaks as one person. This requires perfect timing, balance, phrasing and harmony in inflection.

6. A narrator can read the poem while other children perform appropriate actions; or silent and motionless characters may stand in front of appropriate settings to create a tableau.

Come see the stars so bright
The night is clear as day.
Come see the heavenly sight
And hear what angels say.

Come to the manger now
To worship the new King.
Come kneel. In reverence bow
And hear the angels sing.

Here in a cattle barn,
Here on a bed of hay
Is where the King of Earth
First sees the light of day.

Come see the Newborn lay
Where cattle lowly live.
Here is the King they say
To Him their hearts they give.

A young boy brings his lamb.
A small child brings his dove.
Gifts for the great "I Am."
The symbols of His love.

There by the stabled sheep
Lit by stars above
They worship where Christ sleeps
And praise their God of love.

After the shepherds went
The cattle settled down.
Then Mary's time is spent
Settling Baby down.

 SS1871

See the wise men coming,
They've travelled, O so far.
They hoped for Christ's coming
So followed natal star.

"Herod, where does Christ live
For we would worship Him
And to Him presents give?"
"Judea—Bethlehem."

The star shows them the house
Where Jesus Christ now lives.
They come into His house
And to Him presents give.

To Christ, the one year old,
They brought their gifts with joy,
Myrrh, frankincense and gold
For Mary's little Boy.

"Wise men," the angel said,
"Go home another way.
Do not return to Herod.
He would this family slay."

"Come, Joseph," Mary called,
"And see our visitors go."
"Joseph," the angels called,
"Hurry, it's time to go."

"Joseph, hurry from here.
It's time. It's time to go.
For folks are coming here
Who will not let you go."

"Mary, bring the Baby.
Our things are packed to go.
We must leave here quickly.
O, why are you so slow?

"Herod's men are coming
So we must leave right now!"
"Yes, yes, we are coming.
To Egypt? Joseph, how?"

"Don't you or Baby fuss.
In Egypt we can hide.
These donkeys will help us.
Here's one for you to ride."

The stars shine brightly down
On village streets so still.
Then donkey hoofbeats sound.
Again the streets are still.

SS1871

CHRISTMAS MUSICALS

Shining Star Publications, Copyright © 1989, A division of Good Apple, Inc.   SS1871

PRESENTING A MUSICAL

If you decide to definitely do a musical rather than a play this Christmas, don't be limited to the seven musicals that follow. If for some reason one of these musicals won't work for your group, why not add some appropriate songs found on pages 66-84 to your favorite play? (See pages 5-38.) Be creative, use additional songs to lengthen the musicals or perform a play combined with songs to create a musical that is perfect for your young stars! Operettas can also be performed by assigning solo parts to cast members instead of using a choir to perform tunes. Any way you choose to present your musical, the following tips will make your performance run more smoothly:

1. Only practice singing during your first rehearsals. The entire cast should learn all the verses to all the songs. Assign solo parts where you feel your cast members have the ability and where it is appropriate.

2. If accompaniment is not available, practice with taped music.

3. Practice the speaking parts in small groups offstage. Have several rehearsals before going to the stage.

4. When first going to the stage to block the action, speaking and singing parts should already be memorized. This will save a lot of time once you start practicing on stage.

5. For multi-class presentations or for very large groups, small children could be dressed as stars, lambs, or additional angels, and assigned solo parts in the songs, using a few measures for each child or group of children.

6. If flats are used for set designs, make them reversible so that you can change the setting from home to stable, from outdoor to palace by just turning the scenery. Also, large cardboard boxes, like refrigerator boxes or other appliance cartons, make excellent scenery when painted. Use simple supports.

SS1871

BETHLEHEM CITY COUNCIL MEETING

by Margaret McKinney Baker

Cast of characters:

Mayor

Four city councilmen

Angels (number determined by available stage space)

Shepherds (same as angels)

Mary

Joseph

Three wise men

Setting: At stage right is a crude table with a lamp similar to those of Biblical vintage. There are five crude stools around the table.

Stage left has one large backdrop painted a soft blue. This is used for all of the other scenes. The only additional props needed are a cradle with straw, a doll wrapped in a white blanket, and a chair.

Lighting: Spotlights for each side of the stage are necessary. Use a white spot for stage right, and a blue spot for stage left. If spotlights are not available, use two mechanic drop lights connected to a dimmer switch.

(*As the play opens, light comes up on stage right where the mayor and councilmen have gathered to discuss certain unusual happenings. They are seated around the table.*)

Mayor: (*Standing, speaking in a stern voice.*) We must get to the bottom of these strange happenings. Let's begin with the loud singing in the middle of the night.

Councilman #1: Indeed! My constituents have been complaining about all that loud music out in the Country Estates. These rich people have moved out in the country to get away from all of the . . .

Councilman #2: (*Interrupting.*) We all know about your rich people who live in the Country Estates. They aren't the only ones bothered with these problems.

Councilman #3: I heard a lot of complaining about the bright lights out there, too.

Councilman #4: Music? Lights? What are you talking about?

Councilman #1: You mean you haven't heard? (*#4 shakes his head "no"*) Well, the other night out on the hillside there . . .

(*Light dims stage right and action freezes. Light up stage left where the angels and shepherds are standing.*)

Angel: (*Speaks from memory: Luke 2:10-12, starting with . . . "Fear not," and continuing through verse 12.*)

Angel Choir: "Hark! the Herald Angels Sing" or "Message to the Shepherds," page 79.

(*Light dims stage left, light up stage right as action continues.*)

SS1871

Councilman #1:	(*Continuing.*) . . . was a lot of singing and bright lights.
Mayor:	We must not let these problems get out of hand. If we don't stop this nighttime singing, before you know it, the town will be swarming with musicians from everywhere wanting to sing all night long! Do I hear a motion?
Councilman #1:	I make a motion that all public music be banned after sundown.
Councilman #2:	I second the motion.
Mayor:	All in favor say aye.
All four:	Aye!
Mayor:	So moved! That takes care of the lights and music. Something else is bothering the businessmen in the downtown district. It's that old inn with the smelly stable in the back.
Councilman #1:	The health department should investigate that. I understand a baby was born there the same night we had all the lights and loud music.
Councilman #4:	How absolutely dreadful! Tell me more about this . . .

(*Light dims stage right as action freezes. Light up stage left with Mary, Joseph, Baby Jesus in the cradle, and the shepherds. Mary is seated with the cradle at her knees. All others are standing.*)

Choir:	"Away in a Manger" or "Mary's Lullaby," see page 71.

(*Light dims stage left; light up stage right. Action begins as light is coming up.*)

Councilman #4:	(*Continuing.*) . . . baby born in the stable.
Councilman #1:	It was a couple who had come to pay their taxes. There wasn't a room for them in the inn, so they stayed in the stable.
Councilman #2:	Bethlehem is too nice a town to have this sort of thing happen. I move that the inn be closed and the stable torn down.
Councilman #3:	I second the motion.
Mayor:	All in favor say aye.
All four:	Aye!
Mayor:	So moved. We will instruct the city engineers to tear down the stable and that takes care of that problem. We've taken care of the simple problems, but what are we going to tell the people about the star?
Councilman #1:	(*With authority.*) I think we can safely say that it was an unusual conjuction of bright planets.
Councilman #2:	(*Agreeing.*) It could be the conjuction of Saturn, Jupiter and Mars.

Councilman #3:	(*Indignantly.*) No, no, indeed not! Don't you realize that's too near the sun?
Mayor:	(*Simply.*) We could just say it's a nova.
Councilman #1:	A nova? What's a nova?
Councilman #2:	(*Condescendingly.*) A nova is an ordinary star that suddenly becomes bright.
Councilman #3:	(*Excitedly.*) That's it! Yes, that's it!
Councilman #2:	Well, I think it's Venus at its most brilliant.
Mayor:	I really don't think any of these things is the answer. (*Goes to door, looks out.*) Look how it actually points down to a certain place on Earth. Almost as though it were pointing out a special place.
Councilman #4:	(*Going to door.*) I noticed that, too. Where do you suppose it would lead to if . . .

(*Light dims stage right as action freezes. Light up stage left where Mary, Joseph, Baby Jesus and the three wise men are located. Mary is seated holding Baby Jesus in her arms. The wise men are gazing at the star.*)

Choir:	"O Lovely Star," see page 84.

(*Light dims stage left. Light up stage right where the action continues.*)

Councilman #4:	(*Continuing.*) . . . we were to follow it?
Mayor:	That's not really our problem. What are we going to tell the people?
Councilman #4:	I move we tell the people that it is Venus at it's brightest.
Councilman #2:	I second the motion!
Mayor:	All in favor say aye.
All four:	Aye!
Mayor:	So moved. Well, we've taken care of all the problems surrounding this situation. Now the little town of Bethlehem can settle down to a nice, quiet place to live once more. Do I hear a motion to adjourn?
Councilman #1:	I move we adjourn.
Councilman #2:	I second the motion.
Mayor:	All in favor say aye.
All four:	Aye!
Mayor:	So moved. Meeting is adjourned.

(*Light dims as play ends.*)

Choir:	"I Am Bethlehem!" see page 66.

Shining Star Publications, Copyright © 1989, A division of Good Apple, Inc. SS1871

REBECCA'S SHAWL

by Anne M. Evans

Cast of characters:

Baby Jesus (doll)	Rebecca	Three shepherds
Mary	Mother	One speaking angel
Joseph	Three wise men	Other angels

Setting: Center Stage: Interior of stable. Pile of straw and box for manger.

Setting A: Left of center stage. Shepherds standing in a group.

Setting B: Right of center stage. Three wise men bearing gifts. House lights dim, or out. Spotlight on center stage with Rebecca and Mother. Mother holding purple shawl.

Scene I

Mother: Rebecca, here is the shawl I wove especially for you. Take good care of it, for it took me many long hours to make.

Rebecca: (*Taking shawl from Mother.*) Oh, Mother, it is so lovely and soft. And what a rich shade of purple it is; a color fit for a king; only I will be a princess when I wear it. I will truly take good care of it. No one in Bethlehem has a shawl as lovely as mine. (*Puts shawl over her shoulders and prances around.*) Oh, it is a very special shawl, I just know it is.

Mother: (*Shaking her head.*) Come now. Enough of that, you silly girl. I made it purple because that was the only color dye I had. But now there is work to be done. Put some fresh straw in the manger and feed the animals. (*Mother leaves.*)

(*Rebecca scatters straw over floor and puts straw in manger. She stops and grasps the shawl.*) Oh, my shawl. I mustn't get my beautiful shawl dirty and dusty with all this work. (*Takes off shawl and holds it up to admire it again.*) It *is* fit for a king. It *is*. I just *know* it is. (*Places shawl on edge of manger and continues to scatter straw.*)

Mother: (*From offstage.*) Rebecca! Rebecca! Come here! I need you to help in the house. Come at once! (*Rebecca runs offstage, leaving shawl on edge of manger.*)

Rebecca: I'm coming, Mother.

(*Enter Joseph and Mary carrying Baby Jesus.*)

Joseph: Oh, Mary, I tried so hard to get a room for us, but everywhere I went they said they had no room. Finally the man at the inn here said we could stay in this stable. And to think you had to give birth in this horrible place. Yet, I guess we must be grateful.

Mary:	Oh, Joseph. It is not horrible. See how sweet the fresh hay smells. And it will make a soft place for us to sleep.
Joseph:	Yes, we can sleep here, but what about our Baby. Where will He sleep?

(*Mary looks around and goes over to manger.*)

Mary:	(*Pointing to manger.*) He will sleep here in this manger on the fresh straw. And look, here is a lovely purple shawl. We will lay it on the hay so our Baby will be comfortable and the straw will not scratch Him.

(*Joseph spreads shawl on hay as Mary places baby Jesus in the manger.*)

Mary:	(*Caressing baby.*) Such a beautiful Child we have.
Joseph:	We will call him Jesus, as the angel has instructed.
Mary:	Jesus. That is a fine name, so gentle and kind.
Joseph:	Yes, Jesus. It *is* a fine name.

(*Choir: Sings "Away in a Manger" or "Jesus Is Sleeping," see page 82 as Mary kneels by the manger and Joseph remains standing.*)

Scene II

(*Spotlight on wise men to right of center stage.*)

First Wise Man:	We have travelled many miles, always guided by that bright and shining star. And soon we will see the little one that is called the Saviour. The angel said He would be wrapped in swaddling clothes and lying in a manger. How very unusual, a Saviour lying in a manger. I bring Him gold; the most precious of metals—a gift for a king. And yet we shall find Him in a manger.
Second Wise Man:	Yes, it has been a long journey, and our animals are tired. How happy I will be to see this babe that is Christ the King. And I bring Him myrrh, the most fragrant and costly of spices from Arabia. It is the symbol of relief from pain He may suffer some day.
Third Wise Man:	And for the Babe, I have a gift of frankincense, which will be a symbol of the Savior's kingliness.
First Wise Man:	But let us hurry. (*Points skyward.*) See, the star shines brightly over the town of Bethlehem, and there we shall find Him and give Him our gifts.

(*Wise men walk slowly to center stage as choir sings "O Little Town of Bethlehem" or "O Lovely Star," see page 84.*)

First Wise Man:	(*Doubtfully.*) Can this truly be the place?

Joseph:	Come in. Come in. We have not much to share with you except the birth of our son who is called Jesus.
Third Wise Man:	(*To Joseph.*) We have followed the star and come here to worship Christ the King. An angel said we would find Him wrapped in swaddling clothes and lying in a manger. We bring Him gifts of gold and myrrh and frankincense. (*Wise men place gifts at foot of manger and then back off.*)
Choir:	Sings "We Three Kings," or "The Wise Men," see page 81.

Scene III

(*Spotlight shifts to shepherds standing together. Choir sings: "O Holy Night," or "O Lovely Star," see page 84.*)

First Shepherd:	How still is the night. The sheep are quiet and above us the stars shine brightly in the heavens.
Second Shepherd:	(*Pointing.*) But look over there. What is that light that I see? Surely it is not natural.
Third Shepherd:	And see how it grows brighter. I am sorely afraid. Perhaps it will harm us.
Second Shepherd:	I too am afraid. What shall we do? What is it? What is it? (*Shepherds huddle together in fright.*)

(*Enter angels.*)

First Angel:	(*Raises her hand to shepherds.*) Fear not: for, behold, I bring you tidings of great joy. For unto you is born this day in the city of David a Saviour, which is Christ the Lord.
Other Angels:	Glory to God in the highest, and on earth peace, good will toward men.
First Shepherd:	Hark! Surely these are angel voices. We have nothing to fear. We must go to Bethlehem and see the Saviour that we may worship Him.

(*Light follows shepherds to center stage where they enter stable.*)

Third Shepherd:	(*To Joseph.*) We are but simple shepherds. An angel appeared to us saying we would find Christ the King lying in a manger. We have come to worship Him that we may tell the world what we have seen this night. (*Shepherds kneel to Babe, then back off in a group.*)

(*Wise Men turn to each other.*)

First Wise Man:	(*Raising his hand.*) We have found the Saviour and have given Him our gifts and worshipped Him. Now it is time for us to go back to our own land. We have far to go.
Second Wise Man:	But what about King Herod. He told us to find the Babe and tell him where the Child is so that he too may worship Him. I'm afraid something is wrong. Herod is wicked and cruel and I do not trust him.
Third Wise Man:	Nor do I trust him. Last night I had a dream that troubles me greatly.
First Wise Man:	Tell us of your dream so that we may think on it.
Third Wise Man:	Last night an angel appeared to me and told us not to go back to King Herod, for he is an evil man and will surely kill the Babe if he finds Him. We must go back to our homes a different way and not tell Herod we found the Saviour.

First Wise Man:	Yes. Yes. That is what we must do. Herod must not find the Babe. We will not tell him we have found the Saviour. (*Wise Men leave the stage followed by shepherds.*)
Joseph:	Come, Mary. It is time for us to sleep. It has truly been a busy night. We will sleep here next to our Child.
Mary:	Such a beautiful night. Such a holy night. (*Mary wraps Babe in shawl. They lay down on the floor and fall asleep. Angel enters and goes over to Joseph.*)
Angel:	Joseph. Joseph. Awaken. (*Joseph half sits up and looks around. Sees angel.*)
Angel:	Arise, Joseph, and take the young Child and his mother and flee to Egypt, and be thou there, for Herod will seek the young Child to destroy Him. (*Angel leaves.*)
Joseph:	(*Shakes Mary by the shoulder.*) Mary. Mary. Wake up. I have something to tell you.

(*Mary sits up and rubs her eyes.*)

Mary:	What is it, Joseph? Why do you awaken me?
Joseph:	I have just had a warning. An angel just came to me and told us to flee to Egypt where Herod cannot get our Child. Hurry. Make the Babe ready. We must make haste.

(*Mary arises and takes the Babe in her arms, picking up the shawl at the same time. Then she realizes she has the shawl.*)

Mary:	Oh! The shawl. Such a lovely piece of work. And it was such a comfort to our Babe. But I must put it back, for surely someone will come looking for it. (*Puts the shawl back on the manger. Exit Mary, Joseph and Babe.*)
Rebecca:	(*From offstage.*) Mother! Oh, Mother! Have you seen my shawl? I can't find it anywhere.
Mother:	(*From offstage.*) Careless girl. What did you do with it? Go look in the stable and see if you left it there. I will help you look for it. (*Enter Rebecca and Mother. Rebecca looks around and sees the shawl. Picks it up.*)
Rebecca:	Oh, here it is. I found it. My beautiful shawl. (*Holds it up to her cheek*) My, how warm it feels—just as if had kept someone warm. Perhaps those people used it—that man and woman with their tiny babe. Maybe it kept the babe warm and comfortable.
Mother:	It's a strange thing about that man and woman and their tiny baby. Just moments ago, a soldier came and asked me about a newborn babe. He said the babe was a Saviour—a King. I told him I knew of no such child.
Rebecca:	But why did you say that?
Mother:	I didn't trust him. He looked evil, and I don't like soldiers. I think he meant to harm the child. Do you suppose that babe was the Saviour?
Rebecca:	Oh, Mother, I *know* it was. I just *know* it. And to think that my beautiful shawl kept Him warm. I told you it was fit for a king. I told you so.

(*Choir sings "Hark! the Herald Angels Sing," or "The Angels Sang," see page 77. Cast comes onstage until song is finished.*)

THE SANDALS
by Marion Schoeberlein

Cast of characters:
    Jarius
    His father
    Angel chorus
    Narrator
    Three or four other shepherds

Setting: A shepherd's home

Narrator: Long ago in Bethlehem the shepherds were the first ones to hear about the birth of Jesus. This story is about a shepherd and his son and could have happened to any lucky boy living at that time.

Scene I

(*Jarius' father is pacing up and down. Jarius looks down at his bare feet.*)

Jarius' father: Do you have a grape for a brain? Why did you leave your sandals in the hills today while we were tending the sheep?

Jarius: (*Looking ashamed.*) I'm sorry, but I just forgot them, Father. The grass was so cool on my feet and it felt good to walk barefooted. I didn't mind not having them until I got home.

Jarius' father: (*Sighing.*) Jarius, those were new sandals. When will you ever grow up? Now we will just have to go back and find them before someone steals them. Maybe someone has already stolen them.

Jarius: (*Looking up at his father confidently now.*) Father, I know just where I left them.

Jarius' father: Are you sure?

Jarius: Yes. If we hurry they still might be there.

Jarius' father: I hope so.

Scene II

Setting: Dark scene with hills in background and many stars. Big white rock in foreground.

Narrator: It was getting dark now and Jarius' father was angry with him for being so forgetful. They walked in silence, but finally Jarius' father spoke.

 SS1871

Jarius' father:	Well, do you think you know where your sandals are?
Jarius:	Underneath a rock somewhere.
Jarius' father:	(*Sighing.*) Somewhere? There are many somewheres up here.

(*Jarius walks a few steps and sees the other shepherds.*)

Jarius' father:	Have you found them?
Jarius:	Not yet. But Father, I hear something.
Jarius' father:	Stop dawdling. There's a big rock over there. Look under it!

(*The angel chorus steps into view.*)

An angel:	(Steps forward and speaks.) I bring you good tidings of great joy which shall be to all people. For there is born this day in the city of David a Saviour, which is Christ the Lord. And this shall be a sign unto you. You shall find the babe wrapped in swaddling clothes, lying in a manger.

(*Jarius and his father fall on their knees.*)

Angels:	Sing "The Angel's Greeting," see page 76.

(*Jarius and his father arise slowly.*)

Jarius:	Father, was I dreaming?
Jarius' father:	No, my son, it was a vision from heaven. The Chosen One of Israel is born tonight.
Jarius:	It's a good thing I lost my sandals and we had to come back. Otherwise we'd never have seen the angels or heard them.

(*Jarius goes to the rock and puts his hands under it.*)

Jarius:	Father, they're here. Right where I left them.
Jarius' father:	(*Smiling.*) That's the second miracle we're blessed with tonight.
Jarius:	Father, can we go to Bethlehem and see the Baby Jesus?
Jarius' father:	Perhaps. I will think about it.

(*As they walk offstage slowly, Jarius carries the sandals in his hand, and the angel chorus is heard again from behind the curtain.*)

Angels:	Sing "The Angels Sang," see page 77.

SS1871

THEY CAME FROM THE EAST

by Katherine D.M. Marko

Cast of characters:

Narrator

Gaspar

Melchior

Balthasar

High Priest

Herod

(*Stage is bathed in bluish light. The soft music of "We Three Kings" is heard.*)

Narrator: (*Standing at side of stage.*) At the time of Jesus' birth in Bethlehem, there appeared in the sky a great star. East of Bethlehem, in a country called Persia, there lived three wise men who studied the stars. They were wealthy scholars and have traditionally been given the names of Gaspar, Melchior and Balthasar. They, too, saw the great star.

Scene I

(*Persia.—Three bearded men in long robes stand before an open tent. Silhouetted on backdrop are the forms of camels. The men move to front of stage.*)

Gaspar: (*Looking upward.*) Such a huge star. It is blue-white.

Melchior: (*Also looking up.*) Yes, so bright and beautiful.

Balthasar: (*Stroking his beard.*) But where did it come from? It was not in the sky last night.

Gaspar: It could be two or more stars that came close together in passing.

Melchior: No. If they were just passing each other their paths would part and we would see separate, smaller stars.

Balthasar: It could also be a comet. But that, too, would pass from sight quickly. (*He pauses, strokes his beard again.*) And it does not have a comet's tail.

Gaspar: (*Moves aside, then sits on the ground, in cross-legged fashion.*) But the prophecy of Balaam says a star shall rise out of Jacob and a sceptor spring up from Israel.

Melchior: (*Quickly seating himself beside Gaspar.*) Aha, I think that might be the answer. The star is a sign that the Messiah has come. This will be important to all those awaiting Him. The star means the coming of their king.

Shining Star Publications, Copyright © 1989, A division of Good Apple, Inc.   SS1871

Balthasar:	(*Still standing.*) Yes, but I think it is an important message for all of Judea, not only those who await the Messiah.
Gaspar:	And since we are Persians and we have seen it, it will have meaning for us, too, and for all the world.
Melchior:	(*Nodding.*) I feel we should follow the star.
Balthasar:	Yes, yes, we must.
Gaspar:	(*Rising quickly.*) When do you think we should leave?
Melchior:	(*Also rising.*) As soon as possible, so we do not lose track of the star.
Balthasar:	Tomorrow right after sunset would not be too soon.
Gaspar:	We must pack enough food for an extended journey, and plenty of water, too.
Melchior:	And we will deck ourselves and our best camels in our finest trappings.
Balthasar:	And let us not forget to bring gifts for the new king.

(*They turn back toward the tent. Soft music of hymn, "We Three Kings," or "O Lovely Star," see page 84.*)

Curtain.

Narrator:	(*At side of stage.*) Due to the desert country, the wise men travel by night and rest during the day. After several days they reach Jerusalem in Judea. King Herod is the ruler of all Judea. He is cruel and mean, old and sick. People say he is going mad. So far he has not heard of Jesus' birth.

Scene II

(*Jerusalem—A room in King Herod's palace. There is a couch, a chair and a small table. A curtain on one side indicates a window. Herod is reclining on the couch.*)

Herod:	(*Gets up from couch. Using a cane, he goes to window and looks upward through it. A high priest enters. Herod turns and walks toward him.*) Yes, yes, what is it?
High Priest:	Three strangers came to the palace, but they were sent away.
Herod:	(*Snappishly.*) Three strangers? Who were they? What did they want? And why were they sent away?
High Priest:	They said they were scholars from the east, seeking the new king. Your attendants did not want them to upset you.
Herod:	(*Shouting.*) A new king! Does not everyone know that I am the king?

High Priest:	(*Takes a step backward.*) They say the star that shone so brightly these last few nights is a sign that a new king was born.
Herod:	(*Shouting again and throwing his free hand upward.*) A new king just born? What nonsense is this? Bring the strangers to me at once.
High Priest:	(*Stepping farther back, nodding vigorously.*) I shall do as you say. (*He exits.*)
Herod:	(*Going to the window to look out.*) The star is already coming into the sky. It is a big star, too big. It must be a sign. But a new king! (*He shouts again.*) I will not have it. (*He goes to the couch and sits on the edge of it.*) I will not have it. (*Rising, he paces slowly up and down with his cane. He taps the couch with cane, then hits the small table a resounding whack.*) I will not have it. (*He pauses, pulls on his lower lip and smiles wickedly.*) Aha, I have the solution. I will find out where this new king is and destroy him. (*He walks to opposite side of stage.*) I hear someone coming.
High Priest:	(*Entering with the wise men.*) The three strangers are here. (*He gestures towards them and exits.*)
Herod:	Greetings and welcome. (*He sits on chair and waves them to the couch. They all sit down.*) Now, if you will be so kind, please tell me what you know of the star.
Gaspar:	We believe the star is a sign of the coming of the Messiah, a heavenly king, and that he was born recently.
Herod:	(*Leaning forward.*) Do you know where?
Melchior:	No, but we are following the star. We are sure it will lead us to Him.
Herod:	(*Smiling.*) I would be most pleased to learn where He is.
Balthasar:	We do not have that knowledge yet, I am sorry to say.
Herod:	(*Leaning his head to one side.*) Perhaps after you have found Him, you can return here and let me know His whereabouts so that I may go to pay Him homage.
Gaspar, Melchior, Balthasar:	(*Nodding, saying one after the other.*) Yes, yes, yes.

(*Herod rises. The wise men rise, bow and leave. Soft music of same hymn, "We Three Kings," or "The Angels Sang," see page 77.*)

Curtain.

Narrator:	(*At side of stage.*) The wise men, somewhat bewildered by Herod, returned to their camp outside the walls of Jerusalem.

Scene III

(Jerusalem—Same setting as Scene I. The wise men are having their evening meal in front of tent. A cloth is laid on the ground with cups and bowls. The men sit around it.)

Gaspar:	It is strange indeed. I thought surely that once we reached the palace our journey would have ended.
Melchior:	Yes, since it is the home of the King.
Balthasar:	But the star does not stop over Jerusalem. (*He points.*) Look, it moves south, down Bethlehem way.
Gaspar:	(*Wiping his hands and mouth on a napkin.*) King Herod seemed both pleased and displeased to see us.
Melchior:	Perhaps it is because he is old and sick.
Balthasar:	(*Nodding.*) Perhaps, but he did look both surprised and troubled when we spoke of the new king.
Gaspar:	And he was eager to have us to return with news of what we learn.
Melchior:	Yes, he was gracious to us, but he looked sly at the same time. (*Shaking his head.*)
Balthasar:	I am perplexed.

(They all rise.)

Gaspar:	(*Nodding.*) Well, we shall have to move on.
Melchior:	I do not think we have much farther to go.
Balthasar:	No, Bethlehem is less than five miles away.
Gaspar:	Then, soon, we should learn of the place where the new King was born.
Melchior:	And we may even be able to visit Him tonight.
Balthasar:	Yes, indeed. Let us get ready to leave.

(They begin gathering up their supper things. Soft music of hymn, "We Three Kings," or "The Wise Men," see page 81.)

Curtain.

Narrator:	(*At side of stage.*) When the wise men reached Bethlehem, they asked the people they met if a king had been born there. No such news, they were told. At the inn, they changed their question and asked if a child had been born in the vicinity. Only one, they learned, and the birth took place in the stable of the inn. Hurrying off, they found the Christ Child with his parents, Mary and Joseph. Offering their gifts of gold, frankincense and myrrh, the wise men knelt and adored the Child. When they came out of the stable, they found the great star was gone.

Scene IV

(Bethlehem—Same setting as Scenes I and III. It is the morning after the wise men have seen the Christ Child. They have just risen at their camp outside Bethlehem's walls and are standing in front of their tent. They move towards front of stage.)

Gaspar: *(Stretching his arms high.)* How wonderful to have found Him at last. What a beautiful child!

Melchior: Yes, to look on His face is to look on love and peace. My heart is full of joy.

Balthasar: I, too, rejoice at the great privilege and blessing it was to see Him. But I am troubled. *(Shakes his head).*

Gaspar: *(Stepping close to Balthasar.)* Is the disappearance of the star troubling you?

Melchior: *(Also coming close.)* Or the lack of a palace maybe? With only a stable for the birth of a king?

Balthasar: No, it is due to a dream I had during the night.

Gaspar: You had a dream? So did I, and there seemed to be a message in it.

Melchior: *(Nodding vigorously.)* I, too. I dreamed that someone was telling us not to go back to Herod.

Balthasar: Exactly. We must take another route home. I think Herod means harm to the child.

Gaspar: Yes, he only pretended to want to pay him homage.

Melchior: No wonder he looked so sly.

Balthasar: Indeed. We will find another way. Now we must prepare to leave Bethlehem.

Gaspar: I shall be sad to leave.

Melchior: And I. But we have seen Him whom we came to see.

Balthasar: Ah, yes, the Prince of Peace. The King they have named Jesus.

Gaspar: *(Putting his hand on Melchior's shoulder.)* It is good.

Melchior: *(Nodding.)* It is good.

Balthasar: *(Looking skyward.)* Yes, it is good.

(They turn and walk slowly back to the tent, as lights dim and the soft music of "We Three Kings," or "I Am Bethlehem!" see page 66, is heard.)

Curtain.

(Narrator steps to center of stage in front of curtain.)

Narrator: And now, a blessed and happy Christmas to everyone.

(Instead of playing songs softly between scenes, choir can sing each song).

GOD BLESSED THEM ONE AND ALL

by Dee Leone

Cast of characters:

Narrator(s)	Brown Bug	Dove 1
Mary	Brown Bird	Dove 2
Joseph	Rooster	Cow
Soldier 1	Sheep	Donkey
Soldier 2	Spider	Three wise men
Innkeeper	Shepherds	Choir members

Setting: A manger crib with a baby doll hidden behind it can be near one side of the stage. A cardboard fire can be laying down nearby so that it can't yet be seen. A little loose hay can be scattered on the ground and a small bale of hay can be in one corner.

Note: The narrator's part can be divided among several children, if desired. Songs can be added. Suggested songs can be replaced by other songs.

Props: Manger crib, baby doll, small bale of hay, loose hay, blanket, cardboard stand-up fire, twigs, some logs (real or rolled paper), web of yarn, gifts for the kings to carry, flashlight, comb for rooster's head, and a red piece of material for the brown bird.

Narrator: Long ago, in a small stable in Bethlehem, the animals were settling down for the night.

Cow: What a day it's been! Noisy crowds of people right outside our stable, continuous knocking on the innkeeper's door, and to top it all off, the innkeeper has forgotten to bring us more food. There's very little fresh hay left. (*Points to a small bale.*)

Sheep: The innkeeper has been too busy to think about us. People have been coming from all over to sleep at the inn. Caesar has decreed that everyone must go to his own town to be taxed. That's why Bethlehem is so crowded right now.

Rooster: (*The rooster should not have on a red comb until later in the play.*) Well, I'm glad it's finally getting dark. Most of the people are sleeping and this little town is quiet and still once again.

Choir: Sings "O Little Town of Bethlehem," verse 1, as animals gather near manger and sleep. Then Mary, Joseph, and the donkey walk past the stable to the other side of the stage where Joseph knocks at the door of the inn.

Innkeeper: (*Comes to the door, yawns, and asks sleepily.*) What do you want?

Joseph: We need a room in which to stay.

Innkeeper: A room! This inn is full. All the inns in Bethlehem are. It's very late, you know.

Joseph: But we *must* have a place to stay. My wife is ready to give birth.

Shining Star Publications, Copyright © 1989, A division of Good Apple, Inc. SS1871

Innkeeper:	Hmmm. Well, come with me. (*He leads them halfway to the stable. He points to the stable and speaks. The animals awaken slowly at the sound of his voice.*) You can stay in that stable. It's the best I can do. (*He leaves.*)
Brown Bird:	Did you hear that? The innkeeper is going to let someone stay in our stable.
Brown Bug:	It's too crowded in here already. There's barely enough room for even a little creature like me.

(*Mary, Joseph, and the donkey enter.*)

Dove:	Oh, no! There's three of them. How will we all fit in this little stable?
Cow:	They all look so tired.
Sheep:	They must have come a long way.
Rooster:	Maybe we should make room for them.

(*The animals all back away from the manger around which they've been standing and sitting. The cow lies in front of the hay so that it is not visible to Mary and Joseph. Mary and Joseph take a place near the manger. The donkey lays in front of Mary.*)

Bird:	Little Donkey, what have you been doing to make you so tired?
Donkey:	I've carried Mary from Nazareth to Bethlehem. She is very tired and is about to give birth.
Bug:	Where did you get those beautiful long ears?
Donkey:	Long ears? Why, I don't know. I didn't have them when we left Bethlehem.
Narrator:	Because the donkey had carried Mary faithfully and without complaint, God blessed the donkey in a special way. He gave the donkey long ears, a reminder of the special, long journey the donkey had made.
Choir:	Sing verse 2 of "Who Is This Baby?" See page 69.

(*Mary picks up a baby doll. The donkey gets up and takes a place near the other animals. Now Mary can be seen with Baby Jesus.*)

Dove 1:	Look at the baby!
Joseph:	It's a boy! A beautiful baby boy.
Mary:	We shall call his name Jesus. Tonight a miracle has taken place.
Joseph:	But where shall we lay Him? There is no crib here.
Mary:	We can use this manger.
Joseph:	But the manger is hard and I see no fresh hay to lay in it to make it soft. (*Picks up a few pieces of straw.*) These old pieces of straw are all I see.
Cow:	(*Moves to reveal the hay and then brings it forward.*) I'm hungry, but I'm going to give them this hay. The baby must have a soft place to lay.
Choir:	Sings verse 1 of "Who Is This Baby?" substituting the word COW for the word LAMB, see page 69.
Narrator:	The cow's special gift did not go unnoticed by God. God blessed the cow. A special relationship still exists among the cow and children today, for it is from the cow that we get milk. And it's all because the cow in the stable could not let the baby sleep in a hard manger, so she brought forth the first bit of fresh hay and placed it there.
Choir:	Sings "Away in a Manger," verses 1 and 2.
Joseph:	Now Baby Jesus has a soft place to lay his head, but what will we cover him with? We have no blanket.

Shining Star Publications, Copyright © 1989, A division of Good Apple, Inc.

SS1871

Sheep:	I need my wool coat to keep warm, but the newborn child needs it more. I will give him some of my wool. He is wrapped in swaddling clothes, but that will not be warm enough in this cold stable. (*Pretends to pull off some wool and then presents a blanket to Mary.*)
Choir:	Sings verse 3 of "Who Is This Baby?" substituting the words A LAMB for AN OX, see page 69.
Rooster:	Woolly Sheep, look! Your wool coat is thick with beatiful curls and waves.
Narrator:	Because the sheep had given of himself, God blessed the sheep in a special way. He gave the sheep a coat thicker, softer, curlier, and more beautiful than the one the sheep had. (*Dove 2 enters and takes a place near the first dove. Shepherds also enter and kneel near the manger.*)
Dove 1:	Who are these people?
Dove 2:	These are shepherds who are abiding in the field, keeping watch over their flock. As I was flying through the night, an angel of the Lord appeared in my path. The shepherds were very frightened, but the angel told them not to be afraid. The angel said that a Saviour had been born. The angel told the shepherds they would find the Babe wrapped in swaddling clothes, lying in a manger.
Dove 1:	(*Points to manger.*) Look! There in the manger. That must be the Saviour the angel spoke of.
Choir:	Sings verse 4 of "Who Is This Baby?" substituting the word BIRD for the word BEASTS, see page 69.
Dove 2:	Oh, the shepherds have awakened the baby. (*Mary picks him up.*) Let's sing him back to sleep so he will not cry.
Choir:	Sings "Jesus Is Sleeping," see page 82.
Narrator:	And so the doves cooed the baby peacefully to sleep. And because of that and because the dove spread the message proclaimed by the angels who said, "Glory to God in the highest, and on earth peace, good will toward men," the dove now has the honor of being referred to as the bird of peace. (*Pause.*) The shepherds stayed for a time while Mary held the sleeping child. After the shepherds left, Mary and Joseph decided to get some rest.
Joseph:	I will build a fire so we will be warm while we sleep. (*He stands up a cardboard fire. Then Mary and Joseph recline.*)
Narrator:	As Jesus, Mary, and Joseph slept, a cold wind came and blew out the fire. (*Someone can nonchalantly knock down the cardboard fire.*)
Brown Bird:	(*Examines the fire.*) Oh, the fire is out. Only a few embers are left burning. Mary and Joseph will get cold and awaken. They need their rest. I must do something to help.
Narrator:	(*Brown Bird performs the actions the narrator is describing.*) The little brown bird took some twigs from his own nest. He dropped them on the pile and beat his wings gently to start the fire again. (*The bird stands up the cardboard fire and backs away. With his back toward the audience, he attaches a piece of red material to his chest. This can be done easily if Velcro has been attached to the original costume and to the red piece of material.*)
Brown Bird:	There. The fire should last until morning now.
Cow:	Little bird, oh little bird. You're beautiful!
Narrator:	When the little bird looked down, he saw that he was no longer a plain brown bird. Because of his kindness, God had blessed him in a special way. The warmth and glow of the fire was imprinted on him. And that's how the plain brown bird became little robin redbreast.

Shining Star Publications, Copyright © 1989, A division of Good Apple, Inc. SS1871

Little Bug:	The baby is starting to cry softly. I'll see what I can do to stop him. (*He moves to the manger.*) Why look! A piece of straw is hurting the baby's head. I'll remove it before the baby awakens Mary and Joseph.
Narrator:	And so the little brown bug took away the piece of straw that had been hurting the Baby Jesus.
Little Bug:	(*Removes a piece of straw.*) There. The baby has stopped crying.
Sheep:	Little Bug, what's that beautiful light on your tail?
Narrator:	The little bug looked back at his tail. It was glowing on and off. (*Little Bug turns a flashlight off and on several times.*) His tail had touched the head of Jesus as he removed the straw piece. Now his tail was filled with the radiant glow of the halo which was around the baby's head. That is how God blessed the bug for his kind deed, and that is how a plain brown bug became the lightning bug. (*Pause.*) It was not long before visitors from afar came to pay homage to the newborn King. The animals heard their approach.
Choir:	Sings "The Wise Men," see page 81.
Rooster:	Who are these men?
Dove 2:	When I was flying through Jerusalem a short while ago, I saw these same men at Herod's palace. They were saying, "Where is he that is born King of the Jews? For we have seen his star in the east and have come to worship him?" Herod told them to go to Bethlehem and then to bring him news of the child, so that he too, could pay the baby homage. But after the wise men left, I heard Herod talking to others at the palace. He has no intention of worshipping the baby. Instead he wishes the baby harm.
Rooster:	Somehow, I must make sure these wise men do not tell Herod where the child is.
Narrator:	When the wise men left, the rooster went with them. (*The wise men leave their gifts near the manger. Then the rooster and wise men move to the other side of the stage.*) The wise men were warned in a dream not to return to Herod. They began traveling in a different direction. Some of Herod's spies noticed this and told Herod. Herod sent some men to try to catch up to the kings. He wanted the men to find out where the Baby Jesus was. (*Wise men recline.*) One night while the wise men lay sleeping, the rooster started crowing very loudly. (*Rooster crows and awakens wise men.*) The rooster had been flying about and knew that Herod's men were only an hour's distance away. The wise men could not sleep with all the crowing, so they packed their things and got an early start. Thanks to the rooster, Herod's men never caught up to the kings. (*The rooster returns to the stable. On his way, he puts on a headpiece with a rooster's comb.*)
Brown Bird:	Rooster, what's that on your head?
Sheep:	It looks like a ruby crown.
Brown Bug:	It's beautiful!
Narrator:	Because of the rooster's kind deed, God blessed the rooster with a comb, like a crown as precious as the ones worn by the kings he helped. (*Pause.*) Herod was angry when he found out the wise men had returned to their land without telling him where the baby was. He decided to have all the babies killed who had been born around the time Jesus was born, so that he would be sure to kill Jesus. But Joseph was warned in a dream to flee to Egypt with Mary and the Child. (*Mary, Joseph, the Baby, and*

Shining Star Publications, Copyright © 1989, A division of Good Apple, Inc.

SS1871

the donkey prepare to leave the stable.) Now all this time in the stable, there had been a quiet little spider. (*Comes onstage near stable.*) Not even the animals had noticed it. The spider had watched as the Christmas miracle unfolded before her. She watched as each animal did something special for the family and the visitors. Now the family was leaving. The spider felt very sad, for she was the only one who had not done something special.

Spider: All the animals have done something important except me, and now the family is leaving. There is nothing left for me to do. I'm worthless.

Narrator: Quietly, the spider crawled onto one of the donkey's saddlebags. She left her home to be near this special family always. (*Spider holds onto the donkey as the family and the donkey move to the other side of the stage, which now serves as a cave.*) After they had gone a short distance, Joseph suddenly stopped. (*Soldier's footsteps are heard offstage.*)

Joseph: Shhh! We must be quiet.

Mary: Why? What's wrong?

Joseph: I heard footsteps.

Mary: We must find a place to hide.

Joseph: Come quickly. We'll hide in that cave. (*Points.*)

Mary: But they're sure to look there.

Joseph: It's our only hope. There's no place else to go. (*They all go into the cave, offstage, except for the spider who remains at the opening.*)

Narrator: The spider quickly spun a web across the opening of the cave. (*Soldiers enter and stop at the cave.*)

Soldier 1: Let's check in here.

Soldier 2: There's no need to waste time checking in there. Don't you see the big web across the entrance. If someone had entered the cave, the web would be broken.

Soldier 1: You are right. Quickly! Let's check elsewhere. (*Soldiers exit and the family and the donkey move to the cave entrance.*)

Narrator: The spider who thought she was worthless, played one of the most important parts in the Christmas story. If fact, had it not been for the spider, there might not have been a story to tell. The spider's web had saved Jesus from being killed by Herod's soldiers. When the soldiers had gone, Mary cried tears of joy. Some of her tears got caught in the spider's web. Because of the spider's kindness, God gave the spider a very special blessing. Most people do not know of the spider's special part in the Christmas story. Indeed, the quiet little spider will not usually be found represented in a Nativity scene at all. But how else can you explain one of the most beautiful sights in the world, a spider web glistening with Mary's dewy tears of joy? (*The entire cast gathers back onstage near the manger.*)

All: Sings "Glory, Glory," see page 67.

SS1871

JESUS COMES TO EARTH

by Helen Kitchell Evans

This short drama is written using "foreshorting," or bridging action, with music. Usually this is a very short time (ten seconds) but in this presentation the scenes could be separated with songs by a choir or congregation singing one stanza of each of the songs selected.

(*Lights may be dimmed in the church and a spot used to center on the scene. "Silent Night" could be played while the characters come into the spotlight.*)

Scene I
Angel appears to Joseph—Matthew 1-2

Eddie #2

Angel: Joseph, I want you to take Mary for your wife.

Nolan

Joseph: But she is with child.

Angela #1

Angel: Don't be afraid. She is carrying the Son of God. When He is born name Him Jesus.

Joseph: I keep wondering why this is happening to me.

Eddie #2

Angel: This Son will save all people from their sins. This is to be so that words of the prophet shall be fulfilled. Do you remember the prophecy?

Joseph: Yes. It said that a virgin will bring forth a Son to be named Emmanuel. That name means "God with us."

all

Angel: So you will do as I bid?

Joseph: Yes. Mary will be my wife.

Bridge music here—Suggested songs: "O Come, O Come Emmanuel," "Angels from the Realms of Glory," "Joseph Dearest," or "Joseph's Song," see page 70.

Scene II
Shepherd scene—Luke 2

Ethan

First Shepherd: I'm getting sleepy. Would you watch my sheep for a time? I'd like to nap a few minutes. (*Lies down.*)

Peter

Second Shepherd: Sure.

Third Shepherd: (*Pointing.*) Look! What is that figure that I see? I'm scared. Let's get out of here.

First Shepherd: (*Getting up quickly.*) We can't leave these sheep. We would never get another job.

aaron

Third Shepherd: Look at all that light!

#1

Angel: (*Coming into spotlight.*) Fear not: for, behold, I bring you good tidings of great joy, which shall be to all people.

(*All three shepherds back away in fear.*)

Shepherds: What?

#2

Angel: For unto you is born this day in the city of David a Saviour, which is Christ the Lord.

Shining Star Publications, Copyright © 1989, A division of Good Apple, Inc.

SS1871

First Shepherd:	Where is he? How will we know this is the truth?
#3 Angel: *Abby*	Ye shall find the babe wrapped in swaddling clothes, lying in a manger.
Second Shepherd:	Am I seeing the same thing you are?
Third Shepherd:	I see a multitude of angels!
First Shepherd:	They are singing—listen!

Bridge music here—Suggested songs: "While Shepherds Watched Their Flocks," "The First Noel," "Rise Up Shepherds," "What Child Is This?" or "What Can It Be?" see page 68.

Scene III
Palace of Herod—Matthew 2

First Wise Man:	We have seen a star in the East.
Second Wise Man:	We have come to worship the King.
Third Wise Man:	Tell us where the King can be seen.
Herod: *Leah*	I am king! I am very troubled to hear that there is another. Call my chief scribes and priests. (*Servant leaves room.*)

(*Chief scribes and priests enter.*)

Scribe: *Kim*	Where is this Christ to be born? The prophet wrote that it was to be in Bethlehem of Judea.
Herod:	(*To wise men.*) You three men go to Bethlehem. When you find the child, let me know where he is so I may come and worship him, too.

Bridge music here—Suggested songs: "O Little Town of Bethlehem," "Hark! the Herald Angels Sing," "O Come, All Ye Faithful" or "I Am Bethlehem!" see page 66.

Scene IV
(*At the manger.*)

First Wise Man:	I have brought gold for the baby.
Second Wise Man:	I have brought frankincense.
Third Wise Man:	My gift is myrrh.
Mary and Joseph:	Thank you for your kindness to us.
Mary: *Janelle*	Will you return the same way you came?
First Wise Man:	No, we plan to return another way. We do not wish to see Herod again.
Joseph:	*This baby must really be special to God*

Bridge music here—Suggested songs: "We Three Kings," "O Holy Night" or "The Wise Men," see page 81.

Ashley
Rachael
Gretchen

Angels
#1 Angela
#2 Eddie
#3 Abby
Shepherds
#1 Ethan
#2 Peter
#3 Aaron

Herod
Leah

Wise men
Abe
Johnathan
John
gift bearer + star
Ryan

SS1871

Joseph:	I have had a dream.
Mary:	Joseph, you are always having dreams.
Joseph:	Well, we better pay attention to this one. I think it's a warning from God.
Mary:	What did you dream?
Joseph:	An angel came to me and told me to take Jesus into Egypt and stay there until further notice.
Mary:	Why?
Joseph:	Remember the Wise Men said they were going home another way. Maybe they knew something that we don't know.
Mary:	Yes, they did say that. Perhaps you are right. Do you think Herod might plan to kill Jesus?
Joseph:	He might if he thought he would grow up and be a King that would take over his throne. He is a very wicked man.
Mary:	Well, then, we had better be on our way. We'll just plan to live in Egypt until Herod is no longer living.
Joseph:	Come, we must be safe.

Bridge music here—Suggested songs: "Away in a Manger," "Joy to the World," or "Glory, Glory," see page 67.

Narrator:	The family did stay in Egypt until after Herod died. Then an angel of the Lord appeared in another dream to Joseph and told him to take Jesus and Mary back into the land of Israel.
	But Joseph heard that Herod's son was now King in Judea and he was afraid, even though he had been warned in a dream. As stated in Matthew 2:23, "And he came and dwelt in a city called Nazareth: that it might be fulfilled which was spoken by the prophets, He shall be called a Nazarene."

Final suggested songs: "All Hail, Immanuel!" (If desired this could be followed with a congregational candlelighting ceremony. The burning candles are then carried out into the night as the choir continues to sing.)

Note: One of the most beautiful services at Christmas is the candlelighting service. There is something so wonderful about going out from the church with lighted candles. (*There should be special small candles available from most church supply houses or Christian book stores.*)

SS1871

NIGHT ALIVE

Play by Joan Minardi-Harniman
Words and Music by Judith Capuano-Schera

(All narrators stand to the far right of the stage when they speak.)

Narrator 1:   We are about to embark on a journey. A strange one, yet very familiar one. A journey back to a simple night filled with very simple people and extremely common happenings. Yet it is a night which has been written about in every language in every land for almost two thousand years. A talented author wrote this real life scene, directed it and even starred in it. You call Him, God.

So let us journey back to "Night Alive." It seems as if everyone and everything in that night truly came alive, and has a story to tell. When you realize that God Himself chose each and every character in that scene, that is not surprising.

The first stop on our journey is the backdrop to the night. God chose Bethlehem to be the setting. Listen.

(Four children walk up to the stage carrying a Bethlehem scene which has been divided into four posterboard pieces. This is the scenery for the play.)

Chorus: "I Am Bethlehem!" see page 66.

Narrator 2:   Our God is a God of special effects. To make the backdrop more spectacular, heaven had to meet earth at Bethlehem. The night sky came alive with other world voices. Listen to the joy of angels that night.

Chorus: "Glory, Glory" *(sung softly)*, see page 67.

Narrator 3:   Enter God's chosen characters in the scene. The first to learn of the birth were simple shepherds of the fields.

(Shepherds enter and speak at the center left of the stage.)

Shepherd 1:   This night is different. I know all about nights since I am a shepherd. It is my job to be on guard through the night to protect my flock from danger. I know—I can feel this night is special. It's alive with something new, something wonderful. The stars themselves seem to be bursting with sparkling light. It's as if they are looking down and are filled with joy at what they see. What do they see?

Shepherd 2: I feel it too. The animals seem to be waiting for a special sign also. See how they are huddled together. Look—look at that bright light! It seems to be getting closer. What? (*He puts his arm up to protect himself from the light and falls to one knee. Other shepherds do the same.*)

Angel: Do not be afraid. I am here with good news for you which will bring great joy to all the people. This very day in David's town, your Saviour was born—Christ, the Lord. What will prove it to you is this: You will find a Babe wrapped in swaddling clothes and lying in a manger.

Chorus: "Glory, Glory" (*loudly, joyfully*), see page 67.

Chorus: "What Can It Be?" see page 68.

Shepherd 3: Come, we must follow that star. Even though we do not understand, we must obey the summons of the heavens. Let us go where the angels suggest. Let us find Him—the Babe in the manger. The Babe who is said to be the Lord Himself.

Shepherd 4: But why? Why would the Lord come as a babe? No, He would come as a great king with legions of soldiers behind Him. He would appear in Jerusalem, not the simple town of Bethlehem.

Shepherd 3: Still—let us go. Surely, the angel would not lead us astray.

Shepherd 4: Come then. It is not too far. Let us hurry.

Narrator 3: Enter now—the beasts of the night. The Son of God is met by animals as well as by man. God, our creator is a God who loves differences. He created animals of all varieties with special gifts for man to use. He gave man dominion over all His creatures. So then it is not strange that the Son of God should be surrounded at the very moment of His birth by the beasts of the night. All were there to softly offer their individual gifts of themselves to Him. Listen.

(*The lamb, the donkey, and the ox are lying center stage.*)

Chorus: "Who Is This Baby?" see page 69.

Narrator 4: God is a wonderful casting director. What man could He choose to take His place in this scene? What man could possibly be the father of His Son? Oh, what special care and what special thought God our Father must have taken to choose this person. Enter Joseph.

(*Joseph enters. He speaks on the center left. Then he takes his place behind the animals center stage.*)

Joseph: This night has been so long, so troubling and confusing and finally—so wonderful.
I don't understand, Lord, why we had to undertake this journey when Mary was so close to her time to have the baby.
(*Excitedly.*) And then—we could not even find a place for her to rest on

this night of all nights.

But finally the innkeeper's wife took pity on Mary and now she, no, they, are safe.

(*Strong.*) Yes, the Babe is born and they are safe. I will protect them with my life, if I must.

(*Soft.*) But from what?

Father, I don't understand. I know it is your will that I take care of them and I will. Oh, I will.

I will use my hammer and I will use my saw. I'll build and build. With Your help, I will make a home. With Your help, I will care for Your Son. I will love Him. I do already.

Chorus: "Joseph's Song," see page 70.

Narrator 5: And finally, the last character of this "Night Alive." The last who in reality was the first many months before. If her answer to the angel's question had been "no," then, perhaps, there never would have been a night which came alive for all mankind. Enter Mary.

(*Mary enters carrying a doll dressed in swaddling clothes. She speaks on the center left. Then she takes her place next to Joseph.*)

Mary: This night—this night has been the most wonderful in my life. When the angel came to ask me if I would be the mother of Jesus, I was amazed. Could I have said no to God? Could you say no to God?

I didn't understand then. I don't understand now.

(*Looks down at the doll in her arms.*) But now I hold Him, my Son. He is so newly sent from up above that He has the fragrance of heaven still upon Him.

Oh, my Son. Every mother that has held her newborn child has held love itself.

But, my Son, what is to be? Are you truly God's Son? We will love You and You will grow. But grow slowly, my child, grow slowly.

Chorus: "Mary's Lullaby," see page 71.

Narrator 6: (*Points to the Nativity scene the characters have formed onstage.*) And so here is the real life scene enacted so long ago. We have looked at this scene so many times before. Yet year after year, we are drawn to it. It seems as fresh and as new as the first time we saw it. Our memories just make it even more special.

The Author of Life is a fine author indeed. He is a master storyteller who adds just a bit of irony to His tale. The most powerless and helpless one of this scene, the best Christmas gift of all times and for all times, is the Babe. The gift of pure, simple love, Jesus Christ, Himself. May that gift be your most special one this year and always. Merry Christmas.

SS1871

I AM BETHLEHEM!

Words and Music by Judith Capuano-Schera

66

SS1871

GLORY, GLORY

Words and Music by Judith Capuano-Schera

1. Here up-on a win-ter's night, in a sta-ble warm and still;
2. Gath-er shep-herds while ye can, through the snow, a-cross the fields,
3. We pro-claim His won-drous birth, Prince of Peace, King of Light,

Lies the sleep-ing Sav-ior Child, born to do His Fa-ther's will.
See your King, the Son of Man, all shall praise His name and kneel.
Joy in heav-en and on earth, love and hope He brings to-night.

REFRAIN

We the an-gels in the heav-ens, sing in ju-bi-la-tion,

Glo-ry, glo-ry, joy-ful-ly we sing;

Glo-ry, glo-ry, glo-ry to the King!

SS1871

WHAT CAN IT BE?

Words and Music by Judith Capuano-Schera

1. Shep-herd boy am I   trav-'ling from a-far,
2. Shep-herds poor are we   trav-'ling from a-far,
3. Fol-low-ing the light   to a sta-ble poor,

I hear voic-es in the night, don't know what they are, And
We hear voic-es in the night, don't know what they are, And
In a cra-dle sleep-ing there on the earth-en floor, There

there up in the star lit sky____ shin-ing o-ver me—
there a-bove a great big star____ shines for us to see—
lies a Babe so peace-ful-ly, a lov-ing warmth a-bounds,

What can it be? What can it be?
What can it be? What can it be?
Who can this be? Whom have we found?

It's the Sav-ior Christ we see,____ What a won-drous sight;

Could it real-ly be? (O could it?) What a joy-ful night!

SS1871

WHO IS THIS BABY?

Words and Music by Judith Capuano-Schera

1. Who is this Ba - by_____ look-ing at me?_____
5. Dear lit - tle Ba - by_____ look-ing at us,

Why is He smil - ing,_____ What does He see?_____
Why do You smile,_____ Why do You fuss?

2. I'm just a poor lamb,_____ gen - tle am I;_____
3. I'm just a don - key,_____ tired__ and grey;_____
4. An ox so hum - ble,_____ yet I am strong;_____
6. We are but beasts, Lord,_____ what worth have we?_____

But I can warm Him all thru the night,_____
Rest-ing my - self here on__ the hay,_____
And I can guard Him all__ night long,_____
That we may stay here near__ by Thee,_____

Yes, I can warm Him_____ all thru the night.
Rest - ing my - self here_____ on__ the hay.
Yes, I can guard Him_____ all__ night long.
That we may stay here_____ near__ by Thee.

SS1871

JOSEPH'S SONG

Words and Music by Judith Capuano-Schera

1. Fa - ther, do You see me?_____ It is I, Your faith - ful ser - vant____
2. Fa - ther, do You hear me?_____ It is I, Your faith - ful ser - vant____
3. Fa - ther, do You see me?_____ It is I, Your faith - ful ser - vant____

Jo - seph,_____ Here a - long side Mar - y,_____
Jo - seph,_____ Pray - ing by this man - ger,_____
Jo - seph,_____ In Your might - y love_____

watch - ing o - ver Ba - by_____ Je - sus._____
watch - ing o - ver Ba - by_____ Je - sus._____
I live as Your ser - vant,_____ Jo - seph._____

(Fine)

REFRAIN

So man - y ques - tions in my mind, so man - y an - swers un - known;
Now I can build so man - y things, hard work - ing man I have been;

But deep in my heart, I know that I am not a - lone._____
Shall I have the tools to build a home that's right for Him.

SS1871

MARY'S LULLABY

Words and Music by Judith Capuano-Schera

1. Lul-la-by, my lit-tle Je-sus lul-la-by, my lit-tle Child; In my arms I hold You gen-tly, in my arms for but this while. The King of kings is such a might-y One to be, but for now, be just my Ba-by, my Ba-by.

2. Lul-la-by, my lit-tle Je-sus lul-la-by, my lit-tle King; You shall light the soul of man with the love that You shall bring. The King of kings is such a might-y One to be, but for now, be just my Ba-by, my Ba-by.

REFRAIN

SS1871

CHRISTMAS SONGS

MUSICAL TIPS

The objectives of music for elementary aged children are based upon the experiences necessary to the development of the whole child. The range of learning runs from developing individual ability, to singing simple songs rhythmically, in tune and with the light tone, to the singing of parts in the upper grades.

Singing develops vocal skills and good articulation. It promotes opportunities for frequent participation in programs. Also, through music, children develop an appreciation for, and understanding of, our cultural heritage.

Many of the fine traits of Christian character revealed in later life have their roots in the experiences of childhood. Worship is certainly one of these experiences.

The music that follows has been written within the range of children's voices. Tunes selected are joyous, attractive and singable.

The songs may be utilized in a variety of ways. Some may be used for solos, others for group singing, either in combination with plays or as selections by the singing choir.

When planning your musical presentation, here are some tips for preparation:

1. Sing all the songs with the children to find out which ones they enjoy singing the most. Let them help decide which ones they would like to perform.

2. Practice singing only for initial rehearsals. The entire cast should learn all the verses to all the songs that will be performed. Assign solo parts where you feel your cast members have the ability and where it is appropriate.

3. If accompaniment is not available at each rehearsal, practice with taped music. If musical instruments (example, bells) are to be part of the performance, have children practice with instruments after the first few rehearsals.

4. If the songs are to be incorporated into a play to create a musical, decide where the songs will be used during the play and practice singing while rehearsing the playscript. Children dressed as stars, lambs, or angels can often be assigned solos to lengthen the play and thus include additional children.

5. Experiment by playing some of the songs softly in the background during narration. Would that add to the quality of your performance? Can songs be played softly before and after the performance to set the proper mood as audience is entering and leaving auditorium?

6. Copies of the songs can be reproduced and compiled into a songbook if you want the audience to join in and sing some songs during or after the performance. How you use the songs will depend on your performance. Be imaginative and let the children help make some of the decisions. Any way you choose to use the songs that follow will certainly help you make the holidays more merry. Remember this Christmas, "Make a joyful noise unto the Lord."

TO BETHLEHEM
Words and Music by Helen Friesen

Walk,   walk,   walk to your na - tive town,
Jo - seph head - ed for Beth - le - hem,

Got - ta get your name on the reg - is - ter,
Mar - y went a - long, be - ing great with child,

Cae - sar A - gus - tus has
Went to be taxed there be-

is - sued an or - der to en - roll each one.
cause they could trace their roots through Da - vid's line.

MARY PRAISES THE LORD

Music by Helen Friesen
Text from Luke 1:46-49

SS1871

THE ANGEL'S GREETING

Music by Helen Friesen
Text from Luke 1:30-31 (NIV)

"Do not be a-fraid,_____ Mar - y,

you have found fa - vor with God.

You will be with Child and give birth to a Son, and

you are to give Him the name_____ Je - sus."

SS1871

THE ANGELS SANG

Words and Music by Vickie Garrison

1. The night was a spec - ial night,_____ the King was com-ing to
2. The shep - herds that heard the song_____ were ver - y hap - py to
3. All glo - ry to God on high,_____ good will and peace to all

earth._____ A heav - en - ly choir_____ rose_____ to
know_____ Mes - siah had fi - nal - ly come_____ to
men._____ The Sav - ior has come to - night,_____ so

sing of His spec - ial birth._____
Beth - le - hem here be - low._____ The an - gels
lift up the song a - gain._____

77

SS1871

MESSAGE TO THE SHEPHERDS

Music by Helen Friesen
Text from Luke 2:10-12 (NIV)

SS1871

AT BETHLEHEM
Words and Music by Helen Friesen

There came a knock on the inn-keep-er's door In Beth-le-hem one
A-mid the low-ly an-i-mals was born dear Mar-y's

night,_____ Out-side stood Jo-seph and Mar-y wish-ing
Son,_____ But Mar-y had_____ no fan-cy clothes to

lodg-ing for the night;_____ "A-las, my inn is
wrap her new-born Son_____ While don-keys, cows and

crammed with guests, No more can I squeeze in,_____ But
cam-els, too, looked on in great sur-prise,_____ God's

you may stay in my stab-le snug, for the straw_____ is fresh with-in."
great-est gift_____ to men was giv-en be-fore_____ their ver-y eyes._____

SS1871

THE WISE MEN

Words and Music by Helen Friesen

1. From the East came Wise Men from a-far
2. Her - od told the Wise Men, "Go and look,
3. In a house the Wise Men found the Child

Search - ing for a King, led by a star,
Find - ing that Ba - by King, fore - told in the 'Book,'"
With His moth - er Mar - y by His side.

Ques - tioned Her - od 'bout the new - born King,
On to Beth - le - hem the Wise Men went
In a dream God warned them to take care,

Her - od shook be - cause he knew of no such thing.
For this spec - ial trip he the star to them was sent.
Not with bad King Her - od their good news to share.

SS1871

JESUS IS SLEEPING

Words and Music by Dean De Field

1. Je - sus is sleep - ing, star - light is peek - ing, an - gels watch, keep-ing the
2. Cat - tle are low - ing, winds gent - ly blow - ing,

Ho - ly Child.   God's light is glow-ing 'round the Ho - ly Child.

SS1871

JOY

Words and Music by Dean De Field

1. Joy, joy, joy, joy, Je - sus Christ is born;
2. Wise men came from a - far;
3. An - gels sang al - le - lu

Joy, joy, joy, joy, on this ho - ly morn.
They were guid - ed by a star. All the world is sing - ing
to the shep - herds who came too.

sing song sing. All the bells are ring - ing ding dong ding.

SS1871

O LOVELY STAR

Words and Music by Dean De Field

1. O love - ly star_____ that shines so bright,_____ you are the
2. O star of love_____ that fills the night,_____ you bring me

bright-est, ver - y bright-est star to - night._____ O won-drous star,_____ O star of
hope, you bring me joy, you bring me light._____ O ho - ly star_____ that shines a-

love,_____ you are the bright-est, ver - y bright-est star a - bove._____ O love - ly
bove,_____ you bring me hope, you bring me joy, you bring God's love._____ O love - ly

star,_____ O won-drous star,_____ O love - ly star._____
star,_____ O won-drous star,_____ O love - ly star._____

SS1871

THAT FINAL TOUCH
Costumes, Scenery and Patterns

On the following pages, you will find suggestions and patterns for making simple costumes, scenery and a program cover. Remember to keep it simple. If costumes become too elaborate and the scenery and props too complicated, it will detract from the overall beauty of the Christmas story, which should never be lost. To keep costs down, use what you have on hand or ask for donations before you purchase anything. Use your imagination! The best source of ideas is right in your own head and the children's heads! Put your heads together, look around, and you'll be amazed at the great costume and scenery ideas you will develop. Getting ready for the performances should be as much fun as the big production.

Use an overhead projector to enlarge any of the patterns found on pages 93-96 for backdrops or stand-up scenery. Trace the patterns you want to enlarge on some clear transparency material and place it on your overhead projector. Then make illustrations as large or as small as you desire. You can project the images directly onto cardboard, wood or whatever material you are using. Children should be encouraged to help create the costumes and scenery for the play.

PROGRAM COVER: Reproduce on construction paper. Staple program inside.

Christmas Play

presented by

Thanks for coming!

NATIVITY COSTUMES
Robes, Halos, Crowns and More

COSTUMES FOR HUMAN CHARACTERS

OPTION 1—In this version, characters use masks and wear their regular clothes.

A. Enlarge the given face mask patterns to fit the members of the cast. The patterns can be found on page 93.
B. Paint or color the masks.
C. Glue the masks to heavy cardboard if they are to be used as stick masks, or to poster board if they are to be worn.
D. Cut out the eye holes.
E. If the masks are to be held, attach each one to a "stick" (strip of heavy cardboard, miniature fence posts, paint mixing stick, narrow scrap of paneling, etc.). If the masks are to be worn, punch a hole in each side of the mask and add loose-leaf reinforcement circles to each side. Then tie yarn, string, ribbon, or elastic to the holes.
F. Add any details desired. For example, foil paper can be glued to the kings' crowns and Christmas tree garland can be added to the angels' halos.

OPTION 2—In this version, no-sew, full costumes are used. Steps A, B, and C contain directions for making very simple costumes.

A. Choose felt or another material that does not fray easily. That way, you will not need to stitch around the neck or other edges. Use material which is about 48" wide. It will need to be about 8' long for children approximately 5' tall and about 6½' long for children approximately 4' tall.
B. Cut a circle in the middle of the large piece of material. It should be just large enough to fit over the performer's head. (See drawing.)

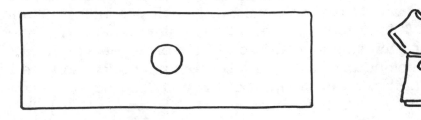

C. Slip this basic costume over the child's head on top of regular clothing. Wrap it around the body and tie at the waist with a wide ribbon, narrow scarf, cord, sash, or belt. Because of the excess width of the material, mock "sleeves" will be formed above the waist. Add wings, a cape, or other details to complete the costume. Suggestions for individual costumes are given as follows on this page and pages 88 and 89.

Joseph, Innkeeper, and Shepherds—Wear bathrobes or the basic costume made by following steps A, B, and C. Use tree limbs or broomsticks as staffs. For a head-piece, use a bath towel or a rectangluar piece of fabric about 2' x 3'. It is to be worn with the center of the *long* edge at the center of the forehead. Hold in place with a sweat band, cord, rope, or fabric belt.

SS1871

Wise Men—Wear a bathrobe or the basic costume made by following steps A, B, and C. To create a layered effect, wear a shorter robe on top of the longer one, or drape a shiny sheet or rectangular piece of fabric over the performer's shoulders to form a regal cape. To make a crown, start with a piece of poster board about 24" long and 3" to 6" wide. Make crowns similar to the ones in the diagram or design your own. Cover with foil or shiny paper. Add sequins, costume jewels, beads, or rickrack. Another option is to glue string or macaroni to the poster board in fancy patterns, and then cover with gold or silver spray paint. Fit the crown around the performer's head and staple the overlapping poster board accordingly. Any fancy box, bottle, or flask can be used to represent the gifts. If these are not available, one gift can be made by covering a small box with shiny paper or by covering it with macaroni and then spraying it. Another gift can be made by starting with an empty plastic bottle. Cover the bottle with short, overlapping strips of masking tape. Then paint with shoe polish.

Mary—Wear a plain nightgown, choir robe, or the basic costume made by following steps A, B, and C. A long piece of material can be draped over one shoulder, across the body to the opposite hip, and then back up to the original shoulder where it can be pinned in place. A veil, scarf, or rectangular piece of material can be draped over the head and held in place with bobby pins.

Angel—Use a choir robe or the basic costume made by following steps A, B, and C. To form a halo, use a piece of gold or silver garland about 20"-24" long and pin in a circle to the performer's hair. Enlarge the pattern below to form wings, or design your own. Use cardboard, and cover it with metallic paper. If desired, attach garland as a border around the wings. Make three holes as indicated in the diagram. Insert a cord about 8' long through the top two holes. To attach to the performer, pull a cord end over each shoulder. Crisscross the ends over the front upper body. Then pull the ends behind the back and insert both ends through the bottom hole in the wings. Bring both ends to the front of the body and tie in a bow at the waist.

 SS1871

Choir—Wear choir robes or dress as angels. An option is to wear a simple choir collar over Sunday clothes. Use a 12" x 18" rectangular piece of material or heavy construction paper. From the original rectangle, cut out one of the collars below or design one of your own. *Important*—The hole you cut should *only* be large enough to fit around the neck, *not* the head. Slit the collar at the back of the neck as indicated. Tape or staple construction paper collars in back once they are on the performers. Use Velcro or snap for fabric collars.

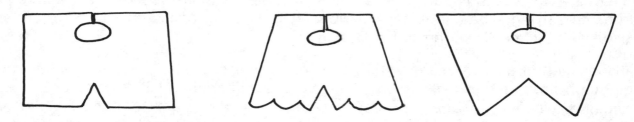

Soldier—Wear a tunic or a shortened version of the costume described in steps A, B, and C. Wear sandals. Use a crisscross pattern to wrap yarn, long shoe laces, or thin strips of leather from the sandals up to the knee. Carry a pole wrapped with aluminum foil at one end to look like a spear. Wear wide bracelets of cardboard which have been covered with foil. Cover a small lid with foil, attach it to yarn or a chain, and wear it around the neck as a medallion. Cover a garbage can lid or a large circular piece of cardboard with foil. Add a handle and carry it as a shield.

Other People—Adapt the above ideas to your specific needs.

OPTION 3—You can use sewn costumes. Directions for fitted costumes for most Nativity characters can be found at pattern stores. Use those patterns, or adapt the one below to fit the performers.

A. With right sides of the material facing each other, stitch the front to the two back pieces at the shoulders.
B. Pin the sleeves into position near the shoulder, halfway between the front and back sections. Stitch into place.
C. Start at the tip of the sleeve, stitch up to the underarms, and then curve and stitch down to the bottom of the gown. Repeat with the other sleeve and side seam.
D. Start at the bottom of the gown and stitch the center back seam, stopping several inches below the neckline.
E. Press material about 1/3" at neckline, sleeve ends, and gown bottom.
F. Add Velcro or snaps near the neckline.
G. Turn the costume right side out.

 SS1871

COSTUMES FOR ANIMAL CHARACTERS

OPTION 1—In this version, performers use animal masks and wear their regular clothes. (Follow directions found under "Costumes for Human Characters," page 87.) The mask patterns can be found on page 93.

OPTION 2—This section contains directions for cape-like animal costumes which require little or no sewing. The capes can be worn over clothing of matching colors and can be used with the masks suggested in Option 1.

A. Choose felt or another material that does not fray easily. That way, you will not need to stitch around the neck or other edges. Use material which is about 48" to 60" wide. The length must be equal to the width. Draw a circle 4' to 5' in diameter onto the material. To do this, first place a small piece of cardboard under the center of the material. Cut a piece of non-stretchable string a little more than half the diameter of the circle you'll be drawing. Tack one end to the middle of the material so that it sticks into the cardboard underneath. Tie a pen or a piece of chalk to the other end of string. Keep the string taut and rotate it to sketch a large circle. Cut out the circle.

B. Cut a circle in the middle of the large circle of material which is just large enough to fit over the performer's head. (See drawing.)

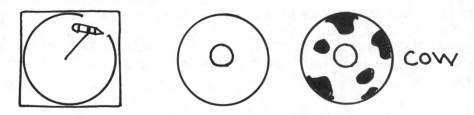

C. Add details to complete the costume. Suggestions for individual costumes are given below.

Sheep—Use white material. Glue on cotton balls if desired.

Donkey—Use brown or gray material. If desired, add a tail at the back of the cape. Make it from material scraps and/or yarn.

Cow—Use white material and glue or stitch on reddish-brown spots, or use reddish-brown material and add white spots. Add a tail made from material and/or yarn to the back of the costume.

Dove—Use white material. Drape the cape costume over the performer. Mark off arm circles. Then remove the costume and cut out the arm circles. Make a cardboard set of wings similar to the ones below. The wings can be covered with white paper or sprayed white. Punch holes in the wings to insert ribbon, cord, or elastic so that the wings can be attached to the performers arms. Cover the wings with feathers if desired.

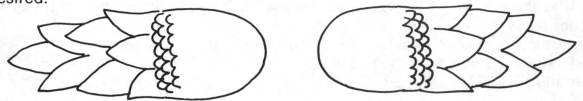

 SS1871

Brown Bird—Make the costume like the dove's, but use brown material and wings. Attach some brown Velcro to the front of the costume and to a red oval piece of felt. The red piece of felt can then be attached to the costume at the appropriate part in "God Blessed Them One and All," when the plain brown bird becomes a robin redbreast.

Rooster—Make the circle costume out of one rooster color. Using material of a different color, make and attach a neck piece as indicated. A set of tail feathers may be stitched to the back of the costume if desired. The ends of the tail feathers should hang loosely.

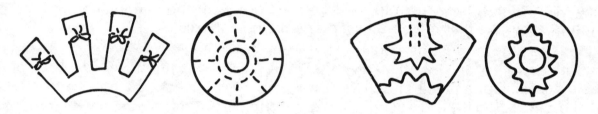

Spider—Use black material. Chalk the circle as indicated and cut on the dotted lines. Then roll each section to form legs. Glue or pin. Then tie black shoelaces or thick yarn to form the leg segments and to keep the material from unrolling.

Bug—Use gray or brown material. Make plain gray or brown wings, by basically following the same steps as are listed in the dove's costume. Conceal a flashlight in one hand and flash it near the back of the costume when the bug becomes a firefly in "God Blessed Them One and All."

Other Animal Creatures—Adapt the above ideas to your specific needs.

OPTION 3—This section contains directions for making animal costume headpieces which can be used with the animal capes in place of masks.

A. You will need to enlarge the three pattern pieces shown onto a piece of felt. The center section should be long enough to fit from the forehead to the back of the performer's neck.
B. Cut out the pieces. Stitch the side sections to the center section.
C. Turn the hood right side out. Make a hem at the bottom of the hood. Insert a 3' piece of ribbon or cord through the hem and pull through so that a piece of cord hangs from each side of the hood.

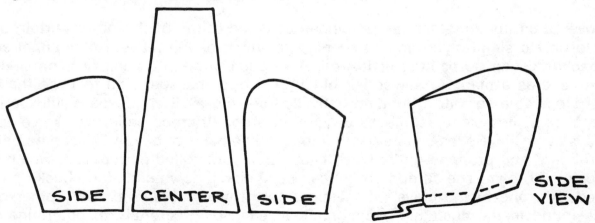

SIDE   CENTER   SIDE

SIDE VIEW

D. Suggestions for individual animal hoods are given below.

Spider—Use black material to form the hood.

Dove and Brown Bird—Use white or brown material. Add feathers if desired.

Rooster—Enlarge the given pattern for a rooster's crown. Cut two crowns out of red material. Stuff while stitching along dotted lines as indicated. The stitches will show, because you will not be turning the crown inside out. Cut a slit at the top of the hood. Insert the rooster's crown. Stitch the extra section of material on each side of the crown to the hood. Do not wear the headpiece until the place indicated in the play, "God Blessed Them One and All."

Sheep, Cow, and Donkey—Cut out appropriate ears and/or horns. When stitching the sides of the hood to the center, insert ears and/or horns to the right side of the material so that the ears will show *after* the hood has been turned inside out.

Bug—The bug does not need a hood. Simply cut a thin strip of poster board to fit around the performer's head. Size correctly and staple. Staple on two pipe cleaners to serve as antennae. Attach felt circles or tiny Styrofoam balls to the top of each antennae.

OPTION 4—Sleeper type patterns, for animals, such as the cow, donkey, sheep, or horse, are available at fabric stores.

SCENERY AND PROPS

Foil-covered cardboard stars can be pinned or taped to the back wall or curtain of the stage to create simple, yet elegant scenery for most of the plays. An optional stable type backdrop can be painted if desired. A wooden crate, a cradle, or a painted box can be used as a manger. A wooden block or a brick can be used to raise the back part of the cradle so that a bundled baby doll serving as Baby Jesus would be more visible. Yellow pipe cleaners, pieces of yarn, or strips of crepe paper can serve as hay if none is available. Boxes can be painted to look like bales of hay. A fire can be painted on cardboard and propped up between two real logs or rolled newspapers which have been painted brown. The cardboard fire can be knocked down and stood back up again as needed in one of the plays. Suggestions for crowns, gifts, and some other props can be found in the costuming section. Read each play carefully to determine what other props (such as flashlights) are needed.

MASK PATTERNS

Enlarge these patterns for use in plays, puppet shows, and classroom displays. Modify slightly for extra angels, shepherds, etc.

SCENERY PATTERNS
Flannel board cutouts
Bulletin board patterns
Clip 'n' copy Christmas graphics

The reproducible Christmas figures on this and the two pages that follow can be used in dozens of creative ways to make the Christmas season more joyful. Here are a few tips for using the Christmas graphics:

1. Use an overhead projector to enlarge for play scenery.
2. Reproduce on light cardboard. Cut out and attach flannel strips to the back of each figure for telling stories.
3. Use an overhead projector to enlarge figures for bulletin boards.
4. Use as greeting card illustrations. Duplicate enough for each child on construction paper. Children can decorate cards with markers, crayons, paint and glitter. Use Scripture verses or phrases for card greetings.
5. Reduce to make patterns for Christmas stickers and awards. (Most print shops can reproduce copy to any size desired.)
6. Use an overhead projector to enlarge figures for a hall mural. Include all the figures in appropriate order to tell the Christmas story. Have children attach Bible verses in sequential order under pictures. Use colored chalk to make soft, pastel pictures.
7. Reproduce on light cardboard. Give each student a set of figures and yarn to create his/her own Christmas mobile. Punch holes at the top and bottom of figures and tie together in a balanced fashion.

Donkey

Lamb/Sheep

Cattle/Oxen

SS1871

Camel

Shepherds

Three Wise Men

Mary

Village Folk

Joseph

Mary on Donkey

SS1871

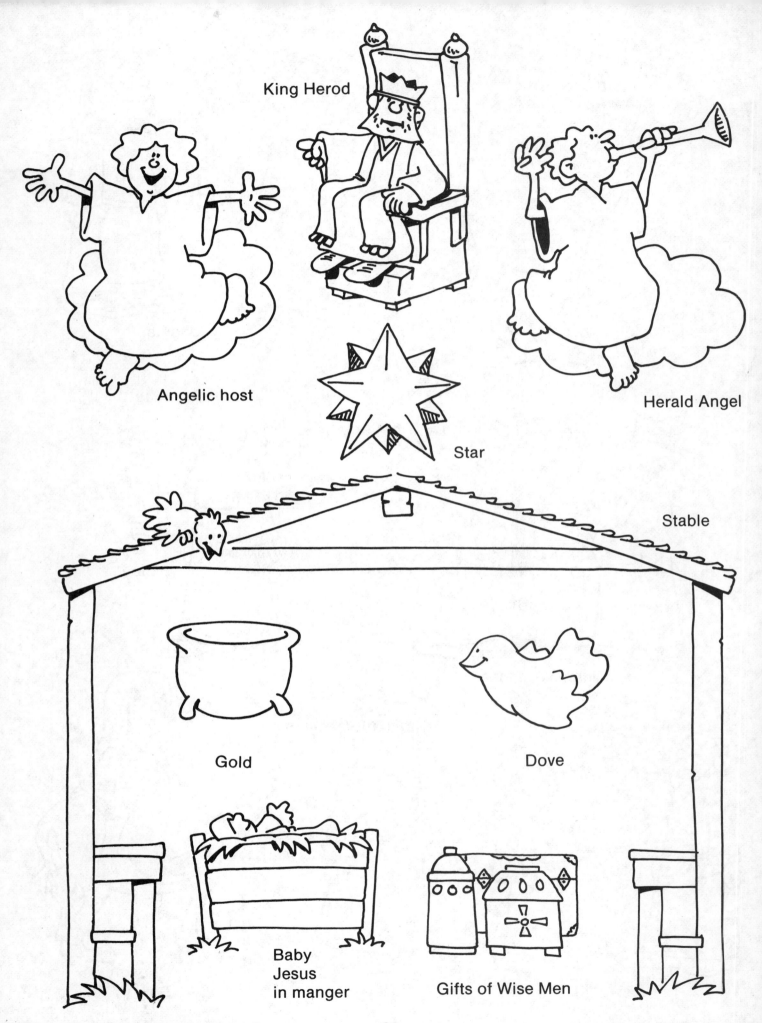

King Herod

Angelic host

Herald Angel

Star

Stable

Gold

Dove

Baby
Jesus
in manger

Gifts of Wise Men

SS1871